BETWEEN
GRIEF
—AND—
GLORY

A STUDY ON THE BOOK
OF LAMENTATIONS

JOY WOO

Study Suggestions

We believe that the Bible is true, trustworthy, and timeless and that it is vitally important for all believers. These study suggestions are intended to help you more effectively study Scripture as you seek to know and love God through His Word.

SUGGESTED STUDY TOOLS

A Bible

A double-spaced, printed copy of the Scripture passages that this study covers. You can use a website like *www.biblegateway.com* to copy the text of a passage and print out a double-spaced copy to be able to mark on easily

A journal to write notes or prayers

Pens, colored pencils, and highlighters

A dictionary to look up unfamiliar words

HOW TO USE THIS STUDY

Begin your study time in prayer. Ask God to reveal Himself to you, to help you understand what you are reading, and to transform you with His Word (Psalm 119:18).

Before you read what is written in each day of the study itself, read the assigned passages of Scripture for that day. Use your double-spaced copy to circle, underline, highlight, draw arrows, and mark in any way you would like to help you dig deeper as you work through a passage.

Read the daily written content provided for the current study day.

Answer the questions that appear at the end of each study day.

HOW TO STUDY THE BIBLE

The inductive method provides tools for deeper and more intentional Bible study.
To study the Bible inductively, work through the steps below after
reading background information on the book.

1

OBSERVATION & COMPREHENSION
Key question: What does the text say?

After reading the daily Scripture in its entirety at least once, begin working
with smaller portions of the Scripture. Read a passage of Scripture repetitively,
and then mark the following items in the text:

- Key or repeated words and ideas
- Key themes
- Transition words (Ex: therefore, but, because, if/then, likewise, etc.)
- Lists
- Comparisons and contrasts
- Commands
- Unfamiliar words (look these up in a dictionary)
- Questions you have about the text

2

INTERPRETATION
Key question: What does the text mean?

Once you have annotated the text, work through the following steps to
help you interpret its meaning:

- Read the passage in other versions for a better understanding of the text.
- Read cross-references to help interpret Scripture with Scripture.
- Paraphrase or summarize the passage to check for understanding.
- Identify how the text reflects the metanarrative of Scripture, which is the
  story of creation, fall, redemption, and restoration.
- Read trustworthy commentaries if you need further insight into the
  meaning of the passage.

APPLICATION
3

Key Question: How should the truth of this passage change me?

Bible study is not merely an intellectual pursuit. The truths about God, ourselves, and the gospel that we discover in Scripture should produce transformation in our hearts and lives. Answer the following questions as you consider what you have learned in your study:

- What attributes of God's character are revealed in the passage?

    Consider places where the text directly states the character of God, as well as how His character is revealed through His words and actions.

- What do I learn about myself in light of who God is?

    Consider how you fall short of God's character, how the text reveals your sin nature, and what it says about your new identity in Christ.

- How should this truth change me?

    A passage of Scripture may contain direct commands telling us what to do or warnings about sins to avoid in order to help us grow in holiness. Other times our application flows out of seeing ourselves in light of God's character. As we pray and reflect on how God is calling us to change in light of His Word, we should be asking questions like, "How should I pray for God to change my heart?" and "What practical steps can I take toward cultivating habits of holiness?"

Eternal

God has no beginning and no end. He always was, always is, and always will be.

HAB. 1:12 / REV. 1:8 / ISA. 41:4

Faithful

God is incapable of anything but fidelity. He is loyally devoted to His plan and purpose.

2 TIM. 2:13 / DEUT. 7:9 / HEB. 10:23

Good

God is pure; there is no defilement in Him. He is unable to sin, and all He does is good.

GEN. 1:31 / PS. 34:8 / PS. 107:1

Gracious

God is kind, giving us gifts and benefits we do not deserve.

2 KINGS 13:23 / PS. 145:8 ISA. 30:18

Holy

God is undefiled and unable to be in the presence of defilement. He is sacred and set-apart.

REV. 4:8 / LEV. 19:2 / HAB. 1:13

Incomprehensible

God is high above and beyond human understanding. He is unable to be fully known.

PS. 145:3 / ISA. 55:8-9 ROM. 11:33-36

Immutable

God does not change. He is the same yesterday, today, and tomorrow.

1 SAM. 15:29 / ROM. 11:29 JAMES 1:17

Infinite

God is limitless. He exhibits all of His attributes perfectly and boundlessly.

ROM. 11:33-36 / ISA. 40:28 PS. 147:5

Jealous

God is desirous of receiving the praise and affection He rightly deserves.

EXOD. 20:5 / DEUT. 4:23-24 JOSH. 24:19

Just

God governs in perfect justice. He acts in accordance with justice. In Him, there is no wrongdoing or dishonesty.

ISA. 61:8 / DEUT. 32:4 / PS. 146:7-9

Loving

God is eternally, enduringly, steadfastly loving and affectionate. He does not forsake or betray His covenant love.

JOHN 3:16 / EPH. 2:4-5 / 1 JOHN 4:16

Merciful

God is compassionate, withholding from us the wrath that we deserve.

TITUS 3:5 / PS. 25:10 LAM. 3:22-23

Omnipotent

God is all-powerful; His strength is unlimited.

MATT. 19:26 / JOB 42:1-2
JER. 32:27

Omnipresent

God is everywhere; His presence is near and permeating.

PROV. 15:3 / PS. 139:7-10
JER. 23:23-24

Omniscient

God is all-knowing; there is nothing unknown to Him.

PS. 147:4 / I JOHN 3:20
HEB. 4:13

Patient

God is long-suffering and enduring. He gives ample opportunity for people to turn toward Him.

ROM. 2:4 / 2 PET. 3:9 / PS. 86:15

Self-Existent

God was not created but exists by His power alone.

PS. 90:1-2 / JOHN 1:4 / JOHN 5:26

Self-Sufficient

God has no needs and depends on nothing, but everything depends on God.

ISA. 40:28-31 / ACTS 17:24-25
PHIL. 4:19

Sovereign

God governs over all things; He is in complete control.

COL. 1:17 / PS. 24:1-2
1 CHRON. 29:11-12

Truthful

God is our measurement of what is fact. By Him we are able to discern true and false.

JOHN 3:33 / ROM. 1:25 / JOHN 14:6

Wise

God is infinitely knowledgeable and is judicious with His knowledge.

ISA. 46:9-10 / ISA. 55:9 / PROV. 3:19

Wrathful

God stands in opposition to all that is evil. He enacts judgment according to His holiness, righteousness, and justice.

PS. 69:24 / JOHN 3:36 / ROM. 1:18

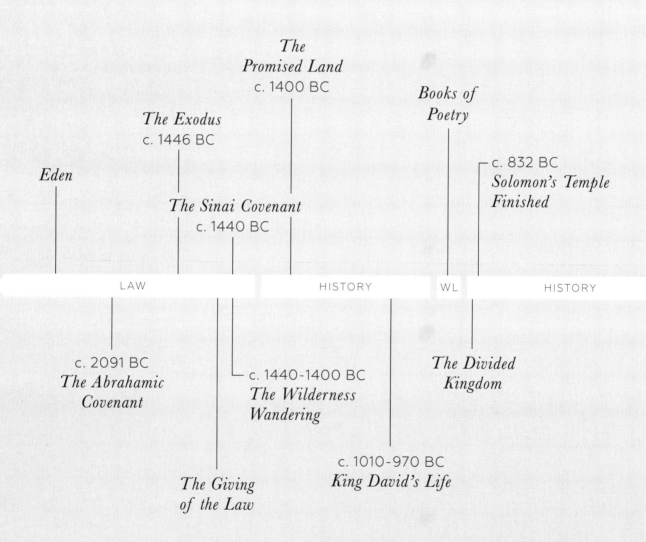

The
Promised Land
c. 1400 BC

Books of
Poetry

The Exodus
c. 1446 BC

c. 832 BC
Solomon's Temple
Finished

Eden

The Sinai Covenant
c. 1440 BC

LAW   HISTORY   WL   HISTORY

c. 2091 BC
The Abrahamic
Covenant

c. 1440-1400 BC
The Wilderness
Wandering

The Divided
Kingdom

The Giving
of the Law

c. 1010-970 BC
King David's Life

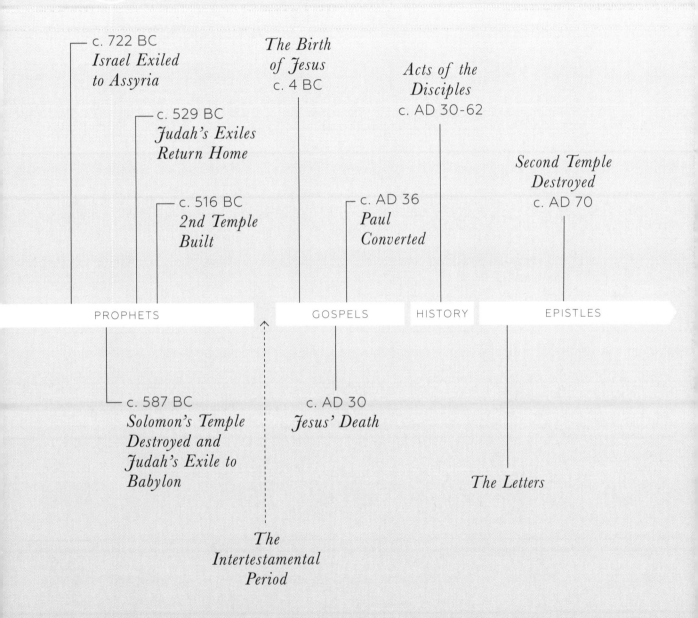

THIS
STUDY

c. 722 BC
*Israel Exiled
to Assyria*

*The Birth
of Jesus*
c. 4 BC

*Acts of the
Disciples*
c. AD 30-62

c. 529 BC
*Judah's Exiles
Return Home*

*Second Temple
Destroyed*
c. AD 70

c. 516 BC
*2nd Temple
Built*

c. AD 36
*Paul
Converted*

PROPHETS   GOSPELS   HISTORY   EPISTLES

c. 587 BC
*Solomon's Temple
Destroyed and
Judah's Exile to
Babylon*

c. AD 30
Jesus' Death

The Letters

*The
Intertestamental
Period*

Creation

In the beginning, God created the universe. He made the world and everything in it. He created humans in His own image to be His representatives on the earth.

Fall

The first humans, Adam and Eve, disobeyed God by eating from the fruit of the Tree of Knowledge of Good and Evil. Because of sin, the world was cursed. The punishment for sin is death, and because of Adam's original sin, all humans are sinful and condemned to death.

Redemption

God sent his Son to become a human and redeem His people. Jesus Christ lived a sinless life but died on the cross to pay the penalty for sin. He resurrected from the dead and ascended into heaven. All who put their faith in Jesus are saved from death and freely receive the gift of eternal life.

Restoration

One day, Jesus Christ will return again and restore all that sin destroyed. He will usher in a new heaven and new earth where all who trust in Him will live eternally with glorified bodies in the presence of God.

IN THIS STUDY

LITERARY FEATURES OF LAMENTATIONS

CHAPTER 1

22 stanzas of 3 lines each in the original Hebrew
{Exception: Verse 7 is 4 lines long.}

CHAPTER 2

22 stanzas of 3 lines each in the original Hebrew
{Exception: Verse 19 is 4 lines long.}

CHAPTER 3

22 stanzas of 3 lines each in the original Hebrew

The acrostic feature is heightened as each line of the 3-line stanzas begins with the same consecutive letter of the alphabet, and the lines are twice as long. This triples the effect (AAA-BBB-CCC, etc.).

The result is that the verses have been tripled as well, with this chapter now 66 verses long but with the same number of stanzas as the other poems.

CHAPTER 4

22 stanzas of 2 lines each in the original Hebrew

CHAPTER 5

22 stanzas of 1 line each in the original Hebrew

This final poem is not an acrostic; however, it maintains the 22-line stanza format of the other chapters, matching in basic form but abandoning the structure of the acrostic rhythm.

LIKE A
FATHER WHO
DISCIPLINES
HIS CHILDREN
FOR THEIR
GOOD, SO GOD
DISCIPLINED
ISRAEL OUT
OF LOVE.

EVEN NOW

Read Lamentations 1–5

Long after Adam and Eve's first sin in the garden of Eden, sin continues to fill the hearts of every human. God has always had a covenant plan to redeem the world from sin. This covenant was a bond of love initiated by God between Himself and His chosen people. God created it in order to deal with their sins through sacrifices so that they could have a relationship with Him. Deuteronomy 28 details the blessings promised for obedience and the curses threatened for disobedience of this contract. The guidelines God gave had to be perfectly met in order for the people to inherit the great blessings of the covenant.

Unfortunately, God's people failed year after year to live up to their end of the arrangement, even though God faithfully upheld His own, while mercifully forbearing their sins for centuries. He warned the people through prophets, seeking to remind them of their covenant bonds, but the people did not heed God's words. They continued in their covenant-breaking by stealing, abusing, serving false gods, and even sacrificing their children on defiled altars.

The time for judgment had finally come, and God's forbearance and warning mercies gave way to justice through the punishment He had promised. Like a father who disciplines his children for their good, so God disciplined Israel out of love. Their punishment was heavy. Jerusalem was besieged by enemies around 608 BC, and then in 586 BC, the Israelites were sent into exile in Babylon. Their king was assassinated, the temple was destroyed, and every covenant blessing was stripped from Israel as God's presence departed from their midst. This is the setting in which the book of Lamentations was written. Although it was written anonymously, the prophet Jeremiah is commonly believed to be the author. But whoever wrote the five poems making up this brief book of lament was clearly a witness to these events.

The horrible suffering that Israel experienced was sent by God in order to bring about justice for all those the Israelites had oppressed in their wickedness. All sin deserves eternal death, and not punishing sin would leave evil unrestrained. Therefore, God's punishment of Israel is both just and merciful. He dealt with their sin, but He did not destroy them as a people, even though that is what they deserved. None of their sin took the Lord by surprise. He knows that humans are incapable of perfect obedience because of our fallen, sinful nature. In His justice, God judges sin, and in mercy, He has a plan to redeem us from it. In losing everything they had, Israel would realize that a restored relationship with the Lord was their only real need.

Throughout the Prophets of the Old Testament, God gave promise that a Messiah—a savior—would come to rescue His people from both the physical and spiritual death that sin brings. The Messiah is referred to as a servant, shepherd, prophet, priest, counselor, king, deliverer, healer and many other things. This sinless one is Jesus. He was God's plan to perfectly fulfill the covenant. In His merciful justice, God dealt with Israel's sin by chastening them through discipline, and He sent Jesus to pay the ultimate penalty so that justice might be satisfied through God's gracious mercy toward undeserving sinners. And because of this, we benefit from Christ's victory too, through the gift of faith.

God eventually rescued the Israelites from their physical bondage to Babylon as well, but the waiting for ultimate deliverance did not come to an end. Jesus would arrive years later to fulfill the plan for redemption by His death and resurrection, but even now, the wait has not ended. While Jesus's work removed the power of sin over those who believe in His name, sin is still present in us. His work is finished, but we will not experience the fullness of its completion until Christ returns.

In the meantime, the book of Lamentations is tremendously relevant for us because we too are living between grief and glory.

We have Jesus's name on the other side of history, but the people of Israel also held on by faith to God's promise of a coming salvation and His plan to fulfill the covenant (Isaiah 52). But the wait is never easy, even though we know that the end is secure, because the oppression that Israel experienced sounds sadly familiar to us. There is sadness, sickness, and pain today, and even Jesus grieved the brokenness of the world He would soon restore. Lamentations was ultimately written by God, and when we remember this, we realize that He grieves with us over these broken things. Godly grief and lament over sin and its damage glorifies the Lord because as you mourn what is not as it should be and long for the day when all will be made right, you learn to hate sin and love holiness. Lament recognizes our need for God and His justice and power over all things.

We will hear these groans of waiting throughout Lamentations, and we may even resonate with many of the poet's sentiments. Waiting often feels purposeless to us, but clearly it is not useless in the eyes of our sovereign God. As the poet wrestles with his circumstances, he learns to remember the Lord's faithful character and value the wait because of the work that will be accomplished in it. The author begins to understand that when God breaks His people, He does so in order to make them new. What the people of Israel brought on themselves—suffering for their sins by the temporary withdrawal of the Lord's tangible presence among them—Christ came to redeem and one day permanently restore. But even as we wait for the permanence of heaven with Him, we can rejoice that He is remaking us even now.

WHAT DOES THIS PASSAGE REVEAL ABOUT GOD'S CHARACTER?

Omnipant. Knows & have to be punished
Faithful to his covenant
Patient - centuries of waiting for E to change
Merciful - kept forgiving sins of the E
Immutable - He never changed what he asked of the chosen people
Patient - waiting for the E to repent

AS YOU READ OF THE BROKENNESS OF JERUSALEM, ARE THERE ELEMENTS OF THEIR SITUATION THAT REMIND YOU OF THE WORLD TODAY?

READ ROMANS 8:18–30. WHAT IS YOUR HOPE AS YOU WAIT? HOW SECURE IS YOUR ETERNAL HOME?

THE LONELY,
MOURNING CITY
OF JERUSALEM
WILL ONE DAY
BE A THRIVING
CITY IN THE NEW
HEAVENS AND
NEW EARTH.

CITY OWNER, ETERNAL HUSBAND, FAITHFUL BROTHER
Read Lamentations 1:1–2

The author of Lamentations begins his first poem with the cry of anguish, "How she sits alone, the city once crowded with people!" The first word of verse 1 is directly translated as alas. It is the author's expression of grief over the events that have taken place in his city. There is great heaviness here as we hear an account of Jerusalem's post-exile, which is their current state. The author begins to personify Jerusalem as a woman in this passage, and he will continue to do so in many of the poems.

In verse 1, the writer speaks of three changes Jerusalem has undergone. The first change we hear about is a city full of people that has drastically altered into a desolate, vacant space. Next, Jerusalem is spoken of as a widow, one who used to be great before other nations. The stark irony in this comparison to a widow is that up to this point, the Lord told the people of Jerusalem that He was their husband (Isaiah 54:5). The poet says that the city has become like a widow because the Lord cannot die; but clearly, He has removed the sense of His presence as a result of their sin, so much so that the feeling of widowhood is their new reality. Lastly, in verse 1, there is the image of a princess who has now become a slave. Jerusalem has fallen from royalty to forced servitude.

Verse 2 begins to tell of the perversions the city has experienced. A perversion is a change of something from its natural form into a corrupted version, and here we see Jerusalem is crying profusely, tears streaming down her grief-stricken face, now contorted and dry from weeping without reprieve. She was once peaceful and happy, but now even her lovers withhold comfort from her. Verse 2 of this passage begins the theme of a griever without a comforter and a city with no rest. The lack of rest will be a theme traced throughout the book; however, God will not leave this need unmet.

There are a few ways to think about the mention of lovers in verse 2. Perhaps the author is just using a metaphor to deepen our understanding of the city's isolation—even lovers will not comfort her, which is a perversion, as lovers are usually a place of solace in grief. There is another perversion present here. In verse 1, Jerusalem is a widow—why does she have lovers? The author may be referring to Jerusalem's unfaithfulness to her true husband, the Lord. The prophets often refer to the nations and false gods that the people of Israel sought after as lovers instead of the Lord, (Hosea 2:13). Now Jerusalem feels the futility of those lovers, because not only are they nowhere to comfort her now, but those nations are the very ones who have taken her captive. Those she thought were her friends have become her greatest enemies and the means of causing her pain.

In these two intense introductory verses, the author has invited the reader into the city's grief and exposed the faults of the griever. He wants his audience to see the contrast between the way things once were and what they have become as a result of sin and vain hope in false lovers. There is no trace of hope from his pen. The poet looks back with regret, because it is only by detailing the fullness of what once was that he can describe the depths of the loss he now knows.

While the author speaks no words of hope in these two particular stanzas, readers on the other side of history can see shadows of the greatest hope that we, as well as Jerusalem, could ever know. Without ever knowing His name, the author of Lamentations looked forward to Jesus, but he knew the promises of what God would bring about one day. We will see glimmers of this knowledge in chapters to come. As readers of Lamentations today, we look backwards on Christ's finished work, and we can see the hope that Christ brings in every passage of Scripture, no matter how grim.

Throughout Lamentations we will see more of these changes of perversion to corruption. But we know that another shift is coming for the author—one we live in light of today. This will be a shift from grief to glory. The lonely, mourning city of Jerusalem will one day be a thriving city in the new heavens and new earth (Hebrews 11:16); the perpetual feeling of widowhood and the tears that plague aching hearts will one day be changed when a whole and spotless bride partakes in an eternal marriage (Revelation 21:2); and the slavery of exile and faithlessness will be changed into family ties as we are made sons and daughters of God (Hosea 14:4; 1 John 3:1).

Our own sin has caused so many changes in our lives—and not for the better; yet by looking back on and remembering what Christ has done to turn our mourning into songs of praise and our many tears to laughter, we can find joy every time we fail. To jump ahead a bit from today's passage, we know that God was faithful to the Israelites, to chasten, comfort, and eventually restore them from the suffering and sorrow that their own sin had wreaked. And He has finally redeemed us all by the blood of Christ—the new city owner, eternal husband, and faithful brother.

AS YOU REFLECT ON THE NEW CITY OWNER, ETERNAL HUSBAND, AND FAITHFUL BROTHER, WHAT DO YOU LEARN ABOUT CHRIST'S CHARACTER?

WHAT SPECIFIC SIN STRUGGLES ARE YOU FACING IN YOUR LIFE RIGHT NOW? HOW DOES GOD'S MERCY IN THE GIFT OF JESUS GIVE YOU HOPE?

WHAT ARE SOME FALSE LOVERS THAT PEOPLE OFTEN CLING TO TODAY? WE KNOW THAT WE NEVER HAVE TO FEAR PUNISHMENT FOR OUR SINS ANYMORE BECAUSE OF WHAT CHRIST HAS DONE, BUT HOW DOES THIS KNOWLEDGE ENCOURAGE YOU TO CLING TO CHRIST INSTEAD OF THOSE FALSE HOPES?

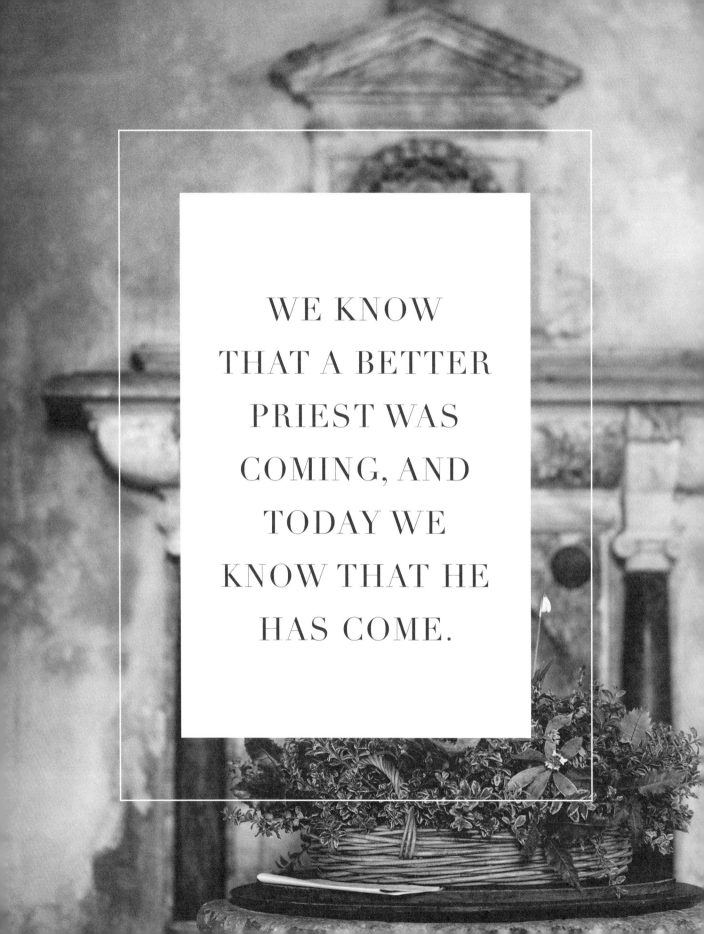

WE KNOW
THAT A BETTER
PRIEST WAS
COMING, AND
TODAY WE
KNOW THAT HE
HAS COME.

A NEW CITY

Read Lamentations 1:3–4 and Psalm 48

The poet is now speaking directly about the exile. The exile was the result of "affliction and harsh slavery." The people of Jerusalem were put to forced labor within their own city even before they were cast out of it. Remember, in 608 BC, Jerusalem began to undergo sieges until the exile in around 586 BC. When Babylon came to take the people out of Jerusalem and bring them into Babylon, they did not take everyone. The wealthy were either deported to Babylon or killed, and the poor were left behind to be slaves and to suffer more oppression in their own land. Jerusalem, the beautiful city, now bellowed under a weight of grief as she saw her people pillaged. She looked on her places of worship only to find them demolished.

A harsh line of irony emerges in the middle of verse 3 that says, "she lives among the nations but finds no place to rest." At first it may not be obvious, but there is a great contrast between these two lines. Now she, Jerusalem, is among the nations—as she asked to be by telling God to give her a king like the other nations, by worshiping the false gods of other nations, and by engaging in their defiling worship practices (Jeremiah 7:30–31). Now she got what she wanted, and yet the terrible irony in all of it is that those other nations she fawned after are the very ones who have attacked her, and now, they are the ones among whom she "finds no place to rest." Getting what we want is not always what it seems.

There is a grim reality in these verses as we think back to Israel's former exile in the land of Egypt and the deliverance they experienced after years of oppression. This time, there is no deliverance. Instead, the years of oppression that began in 608 BC only heightens in 586 BC when they are exiled instead of delivered. Rather than dwelling in the Promised Land, they have been cast out of it and sent back to live among the nations. Instead of witnessing their enemies extinguished in the Red Sea as in the Exodus from Egypt, all Jerusalem's "pursuers have overtaken her."

Back in Jerusalem, the grief of the personified city and of the people inside her is almost tangible. The very city roads mourn because none of the usual travelers approach the city for the religious festivals of celebration that would normally take place. No one comes to celebrate and worship the Lord. When they should be bursting with joyful worshipers who have traveled to praise the Lord in Zion, the gates are empty. The priests, who would normally facilitate these festival celebrations and lead the people in worship, groan in anguish. The young women, who would have sung and been prominent in the joyful nature of these festivals, grieve instead of rejoice.

Psalm 48 describes the usual ascent of God's people into Jerusalem as they would come to worship in Zion; the name itself is a sign of worship for God's people. In Lamentations 1:4, the road to Zion mourns over its emptiness. As you read Psalm 48, hear the confidence that the author has in God's protection of their city. The psalmist praises the city, not as an idol but because it held the temple where God met with His people. Within the city walls, "God is known as a stronghold" (Psalm 48:3b). God promises in the final verse of this psalm that "he will always lead us." How can this psalm be read with clarity when we mourn with Jerusalem today in our passage? With the overwhelming sadness and sorrow of the lamenting poet's stanzas, how can we see the truth of this psalm?

God is faithful to keep His promises, and the poet, even in his tremendous pain, knew that too. He had foretold the destruction that unfolds in the books of Jeremiah and Lamentations (Deuteronomy 28:64–67), and the reality of it was proof of God's covenant-keeping faithfulness. Sometimes the Lord's faithfulness is demonstrated in discipline, as He faithfully trains us in the ways of righteousness.

As we read of their wretched pain and unbearable grief, we see the restless and rest-less people of Israel. In the verses of this brief book, at this specific point in history, Jerusalem feels as though she has no comforter. She is in need of deliverance from her pursuers and yet wholly unable to deliver herself. She is cast out from the Lord's presence she once found in the temple, and not even the priests can heal her wounds. This exile was another type of the very first exile out of Eden when sin entered the world and is the same kind of alienation from God that people live in who do not know Jesus. Jerusalem, with its temple and priests, had been a partial restoration of what we lost when we left Eden.

But we know that a better priest was coming, and today we know that He has come (Hebrews 4:14–16). Jesus was and is the only remedy because only He can end exile forever and give rest to weary souls by the lightness of His yoke (Matthew 11:28). If you feel uncomfortable in the suffering that you are experiencing, know that Jesus is present with you and that if you are in Him, you are never without comfort, even if your physical suffering continues. One day, because of Christ's work as our Great High Priest, every feeling of exile experienced will end forever, and we will live in a new, indestructible city that we will never have to leave.

Jesus was and is the only remedy.

WHAT DOES THIS PASSAGE REVEAL ABOUT GOD'S CHARACTER?

HOW DOES GOD'S FAITHFULNESS TO ISRAEL IN BOTH MERCIFUL AND HARD WAYS ENCOURAGE YOU IN YOUR OWN WALK WITH HIM?

MEDITATE ON PSALM 48. VERSE 14 SAYS, "HE WILL GUIDE US FOREVER." HOW HAS GOD BEEN GUIDING HIS PEOPLE FOREVER? IN WHAT WAYS HAS HE BEEN GUIDING YOUR LIFE?

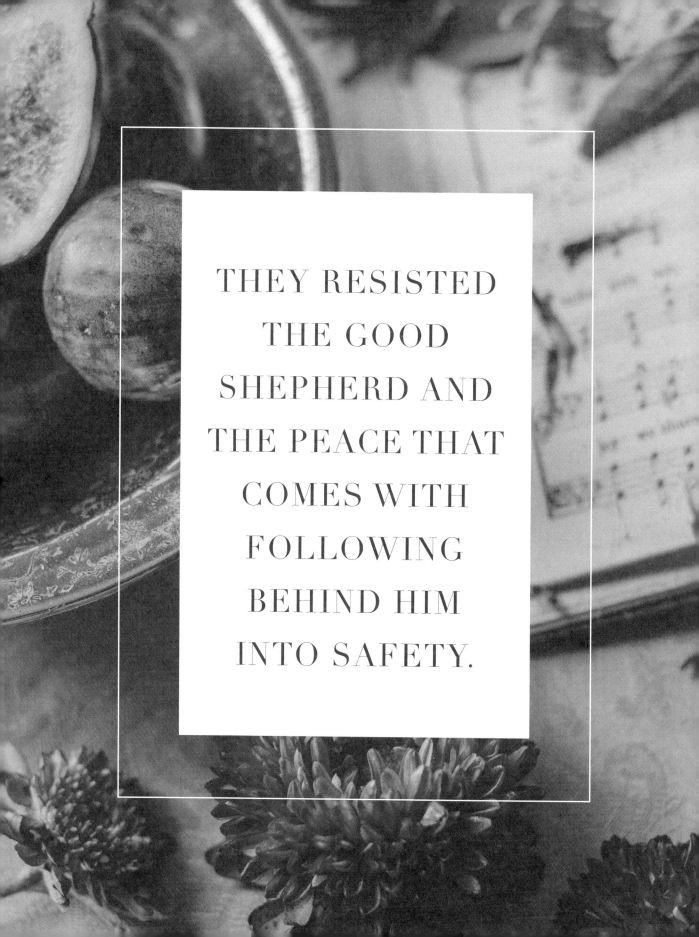

THEY RESISTED THE GOOD SHEPHERD AND THE PEACE THAT COMES WITH FOLLOWING BEHIND HIM INTO SAFETY.

THERE ARE NO CURSES LEFT

Read Lamentations 1:5–7

In today's passage, there are a variety of parties responsible for the grief that Jerusalem, the daughter of Zion, is experiencing. Jerusalem was being ruled by her adversaries. During the exile, there was no king in Judah. The oppressive enemies who destroyed her city had become her new masters; however, verse 5 reveals that it was really the Lord who had brought all of this upon Jerusalem. The author does not try to hide the fact that "the Lord has made her suffer." But why has He done this? She has suffered "because of her many transgressions." Jerusalem had sinned greatly against the Lord and against His covenant with her (Jeremiah 7).

As a result, the city suffered sieges and then exile. Its children were led away as captives, prodded forward by callous enemies. The Lord removed His presence from their temple, which was the most serious consequence of the people's sin against God. Remember, Zion is a symbol of worship, which would have taken place in the temple. The splendor that had vanished, probably refers to the Lord's presence, as it does elsewhere in Scripture (Isaiah 2:10). Jerusalem's leaders, the symbol of her regality and prowess, have become weak and even exhausted. They cannot defeat or even face her enemies, and instead they stumble off, prodded by their pursuers and hunted like animals.

There is a common theme of being before the enemy at the end of verses 5 and 6. Rather than following behind a gentle shepherd and being led to the safety of still waters and green pastures, we hear the subversion of Psalm 23. Jerusalem is in front of their enemy, as if at the end of a spear. They resisted the Good Shepherd and the peace that comes with following behind Him into safety. Instead, in seeking their own glory and wealth before other nations, they found only sorrow. They are before those nations now, and yet their eyes are dark from weeping, their stomachs are empty because "they find no pasture," and their backs are sore from the slavery they have chosen. Resisting the Good Shepherd always ends in despair.

In distress, personified Jerusalem remembers former times. She looks back on the precious gifts that came when she walked in covenant obedience to the Lord. The end of verse 7 tells us that the very people she had trusted instead of the Lord are now laughing over her downfall. The reality is that the people of Israel had brought this disaster upon themselves, because in being unfaithful, they rightfully reaped the curses of God's covenant with them.

Israel had to face the punishment for their sins, at least in a partial way, because Christ had not yet come. Oh, but He was on His way. Now that He has come, there is no punishment left for those of us who have believed in Jesus as our Savior, and the fullness of Israel's deserved punishment has been laid on Him, for those who had put their faith in the hope of the Promised One. Jesus, God the Son, came and perfectly fulfilled the covenant, or treaty—He lived up to every expectation, and He broke none of God the Father's commandments. Now that the covenant is fulfilled, even though we still struggle with sin because of our weak flesh here on earth, there are no more curses or penalties. Jesus has borne them in full. Punishment for our sins is no longer a reality that we have to live in fear of if we have trusted in Christ.

Of course, there are still consequences for sin, by virtue of God's design of the world and the way that His justice is a natural part of its order. But these consequences are never divine punishment. In Hebrews 12:6, the author tells us that "the Lord disciplines the one He loves," but this type of discipline does not deal with sin in a punitive way. This discipline is carried out by the merciful and kind hand of the Father who wants to reveal sin so that He might guide you into repentance—which means turning away from that sin and toward Him instead. He chastens the one whom He loves. He is refining you to look more like Jesus who has dealt with all your sin completely.

Do you ever see hardship and suffering in your life as a way that God is punishing you for something that you have done? God may be shaping or molding you through trials (1 Peter 4:12–19), but if you are in Christ, there is no punishment left for you to face. Seeking things on earth instead of God will always lead to pain, but the Good Shepherd invites you to follow Him and find life and peace despite your past and present failures.

Punishment for our sins is no longer a reality that we have to live in fear of if we have trusted in Christ.

WHAT DOES THIS PASSAGE TEACH YOU ABOUT GOD'S CHARACTER?

WHAT TRIALS IN YOUR LIFE HAVE YOU LABELED AS PUNISHMENTS? HOW DO YOU NEED TO CHANGE THE WAY YOU SEE THESE TRIALS IN LIGHT OF THE GOSPEL?

READ PSALM 46. WHAT DID LADY JERUSALEM FORFEIT WHEN SHE REJECTED THE LORD OF HOSTS?

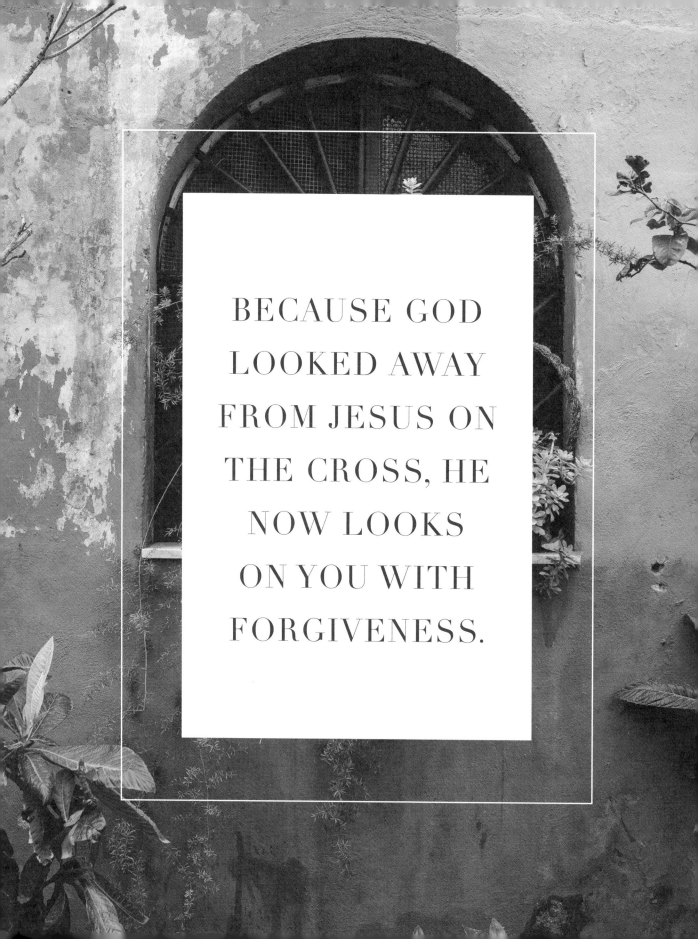

BECAUSE GOD
LOOKED AWAY
FROM JESUS ON
THE CROSS, HE
NOW LOOKS
ON YOU WITH
FORGIVENESS.

NO COMFORT
Read Lamentations 1:8–9 and Ezekiel 16:1–43

We have heard the full reason for Jerusalem's wretched downfall: she sinned willfully and without remorse (Jeremiah 8:12). Not only is her sin severe, but it has caused grief both to the Lord and to herself. Ezekiel 11 gives a glimpse into her sin. Some chapters later, Ezekiel 16 gives the metaphor of an unclothed woman, referring in a literal sense to the city that has lost its walls and is left completely vulnerable.

Jerusalem had become filthy in the eyes of the surrounding nations because of her sins. Those who once looked in honor at Jerusalem now revile her. The author says she is naked, which was a cultural symbol of uncleanness and cause for great shame. This imagery reminds us of Eden when the first sin took place, and its culprits tried to cover their shame with whatever they could find. Jerusalem has been uncovered.

In a beautiful declaration of love in Ezekiel 16:8, the Lord reminds Israel that He Himself had once been their covering. Before all of this torture and lament, when there was peace, the Lord had been the covering for their sin. He had covenanted with them and made them His own, taking away their reproach. God did this in Eden as well. Adam and Eve's sin caused them shame over their nakedness then too. Sin always leads to guilt and shame. But now, Israel had thrown off God's covering in their rebellious sin. They wanted the blessings of His covenant but without the faithfulness that He asked of them. As a result, when Jerusalem fell, there was no one to help her up. In arrogant ignorance, she thought she had made herself beautiful and that on her own merit, she could draw the nations in to honor her. Truly, she brought only shame upon herself (Jeremiah 7:19).

Jerusalem's shame upon realizing the vileness of her uncovered appearance is so overwhelming that she cannot even stand to look at herself. Imagine feeling a shame so consuming that even your reflection in the mirror makes you weep, or maybe this feeling is familiar because you have experienced similar shame. This is Jerusalem's new reality.

The cause of her humiliation is from within her own skirts. The author is likely using a metaphor of menstruation here, which by ceremonial law would have made a woman unclean during that time. Rather than abiding by the Lord's necessary guidance to deal with this impurity, the people of Israel did not consider their end. They did not think about the consequences of their rebellion, and now they have become defiled.

Jerusalem has been an unfaithful and unjust bride as we read in Ezekiel 16. The Lord warned Israel of their fate through the prophets, but His people paid no mind to their impending calamity, and so "her downfall was astonishing." Astonishing? How could it have taken her by surprise? Had the Lord not warned the people of Jerusalem what would happen if they did not heed His instruction? He had, and they had ignored the voice of their bridegroom (Jeremiah 7:21–26). As a result, Jerusalem and the nations around her look in utter shock and astonishment at her fall from the holy city of the God of Israel, to a stricken woman who bears no resemblance to the bride she once knew.

Rejected by the nations she once loved and having told of her grief to anyone who will listen, personified Jerusalem faces the reality that she has no one to turn to, except back to the husband whom she has forsaken. Despondent, she raises her voice to cry out to the Lord. This is the first time we hear words directly from Jerusalem herself, almost as if the pressure has been welling up inside her as she cried, "No comfort! No comfort!" wherever she looked. Jerusalem finally burst with a plea to the Lord. Her pleading with the nations yielded only terror and humiliation, but a cry to the Lord is the first step in acknowledging God as the only possible source of her sustenance and eventual rescue.

Jerusalem wants the Lord to look because the enemy boasts. Regardless of her wayward status, Jerusalem's enemies are the Lord's enemies, just as our own adversaries are the Lord's too. The woman pleads with the Lord to look for the sake of His own name, because in mocking her, the nations also mock God. We can pattern our prayers in this way at times as well. Israel's disgrace, and ours, reflects on Yahweh because we have been called by His name—as His people. The weeping city-woman calls upon the Lord's justice in her request as well. As much as Israel has been unjust in her vile sins, these nations are now reaping even greater horrors among God's own people. Jerusalem's shame has led her to humble herself before God, which is one of the only beneficial outcomes of shame.

In Isaiah 53, we hear of one whose suffering was remarkably similar to Jerusalem's. While Israel's pain accomplished only their humiliation, the tribulation of this servant reaped tremendous blessing, and His work removed all of Israel's shame. The servant in Isaiah 53 is Jesus. The weight of shame that sin causes in your life, by your own sin or the sin of others against you, can only be lifted by Jesus Christ. He came and endured the greatest shame—the cross (Hebrews 12:2). As Israel calls out here for God to look, we know that He was already looking on them with eyes that had planned their eternal deliverance long ago. And because God looked away from Jesus on the cross, He now looks on you with forgiveness. He has dealt with all your shame, so you can ask Him for help and comfort as you wrestle with its lingering effects in your heart. He will not leave you comfortless.

WHAT DOES EZEKIEL 16 REVEAL ABOUT GOD'S CHARACTER? WHAT DOES IT REVEAL ABOUT ISRAEL'S SIN?

HAVE YOU EVER FELT SHAME LIKE THE DESCRIPTION OF JERUSALEM'S SHAME? HOW HAS JESUS DEALT WITH ANY NEED FOR SHAME?

(1) How very long he tolerated Jer. abdomin al behaviors

(2) Generosity at Jer beginning

READ ISAIAH 53. THIS PROPHECY IS ABOUT CHRIST, THE SUFFERING SERVANT. LIST THE SIMILARITIES BETWEEN THE DESCRIPTIONS OF SUFFERING THAT THIS SUFFERING SERVANT AND REBELLIOUS JERUSALEM WILL EXPERIENCE. (SEE CHART ON PAGE 187)

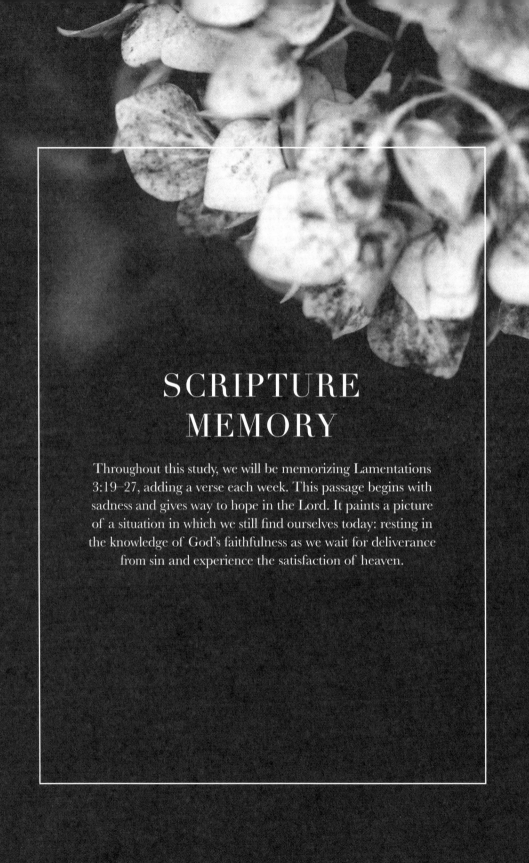

SCRIPTURE MEMORY

Throughout this study, we will be memorizing Lamentations 3:19–27, adding a verse each week. This passage begins with sadness and gives way to hope in the Lord. It paints a picture of a situation in which we still find ourselves today: resting in the knowledge of God's faithfulness as we wait for deliverance from sin and experience the satisfaction of heaven.

Remember my affliction and my homelessness, the wormwood and the poison. I continually remember them and have become depressed. Yet I call this to mind, and therefore I have hope: Because of the Lord's faithful love we do not perish, for his mercies never end. They are new every morning; great is your faithfulness! I say, "The Lord is my portion, therefore I will put my hope in him."

—

LAMENTATIONS 3:19–24

LAMENTATIONS 3:19

Remember my affliction and my homelessness, the wormwood and the poison.

Week One Reflection

REVIEW LAMENTATIONS 1:1–9

Paraphrase the passage from this week.

_____
_____
_____
_____
_____
_____
_____
_____
_____
_____
_____
_____
_____
_____

What did you observe from this week's text about God and His character?

_____
_____
_____
_____
_____
_____
_____

What does this week's passage reveal about the condition of mankind and about yourself?

How does this passage point to the gospel?

How should you respond to this passage? What is the personal application?

What specific action steps can you take this week to apply this passage?

OUR SIN DESERVES GOD'S WRATH, BUT IN HIS LOVE AND COMPASSION, HE SENT HIS SON TO TAKE OUR PLACE.

GRIEF THAT LEADS TO RIGHTEOUSNESS

Read Deuteronomy 28; Jeremiah 52:4–19; Lamentations 1:10–11

Throughout Scripture, wayward Israel is often referred to as a prostitute, just as we studied last week. This imagery is not used in a literal sense but describes the nation's unfaithfulness to the Lord, His covenants, and His commands. Israel chose to follow after the gods of other nations and prostitute herself to them. Like Ezekiel, the prophet Hosea spoke about this sin pattern. In Hosea 4:12, he declared on the Lord's behalf, "My people consult their wooden idols, and their divining rods inform them. For a spirit of promiscuity leads them astray; they act promiscuously in disobedience to their God." God saw Israel's disobedience as a betrayal, defilement, and blatant disrespect of His love and care. But even though the nation was unfaithful and discipline awaited, God would remain ever faithful to His plan of redemption.

In our first week of study, the author of Lamentations shared the details of Israel's uncleanness, and today as we study verses 10–11, we glimpse God's promised discipline on His people through the destruction of Jerusalem and the temple. Verse 10 recounts some of the events of the siege and exile that Jerusalem undergoes at the hand of Babylon. Babylon was God's chosen instrument to bring about Israel's discipline (Jeremiah 25:9). And from c. 605 BC to c. 586 BC, Babylon besieged the southern kingdom of Judah three times. It was during the first siege that the prophet Daniel was taken to Babylon to live in King Nebuchadnezzar's palace. And during the second siege, the prophet Ezekiel was taken to a region just outside of Babylon where he prophesied to his fellow exiles. During each of these two sieges, the outlying cities and strongholds were destroyed, leaving Jerusalem defenseless and seemingly alone.

When King Nebuchadnezzar returned for the third and final time, he besieged the city for over a year. When the city finally falls, Lamentations 1:10 states that all of Jerusalem's precious belongings have been seized and the forbidden nations have entered the sanctuary, or temple. Jeremiah 52 details the destruction of the city and the temple. All that Israel has held dear—her people, her king, their homes, gold, silver, bronze, and the temple—have been either carried away or burned. The items that they have placed their trust in are gone, and all that remains is the God they have ignored and taken for granted—their God who has warned them about the curses they will face if they choose disobedience.

Even though the atrocities that the people of Jerusalem have faced are horrible, they should not come as a surprise. Many years before, in Deuteronomy 28, God warned the nation of Israel, through Moses, of the blessings they would enjoy if they were obedient and followed Him or the curses they must endure for their disobedience. This message was delivered to the nation after forty years of wandering in the wilderness.

God brought the Israelites to the edge of the Jordan River, and before they crossed over to take possession of the Promised Land, Moses gave them final instructions and reminded them of God's law and covenant promises. These were passed down from generation to generation. Deuteronomy 28:1–7 describes the many blessings God would pour out, not only on the people but on their land, crops, animals, and cities. These blessings would rain down in abundance — all that God required from Israel was obedience, devotion, and worship of Him alone. It was in the Lord that Israel would find true abundance.

As we have studied Lamentations, we quickly realize that Israel has not practiced obedience. Rather, disobedience and idolatry have reigned in the hearts of God's people, and the curses and consequences found in Deuteronomy 28 are fulfilled through the sieges and invasion of Babylon. Not only would the nation face exile, but the land, crops, animals, and cities would be destroyed. We see this fulfilled in Jeremiah 52 and in Lamentations 1.

Israel's sin had far-reaching effects, and their rebellion led to exile and the loss of the Promised Land. Moses provided the reason for their discipline thousands of years before when he said on the Lord's behalf in Deuteronomy 28:45–46, "All these curses will come, pursue, and overtake you until you are destroyed, since you did not obey the LORD your God and keep the commands and statutes he gave you. These curses will be a sign and a wonder against you and your descendants forever." Even today, we learn from God's discipline of Israel.

God's discipline always has a purpose. In Lamentations 1:11, we read that the people cry out to the Lord to see them in their despised state. God has never left them, but through His discipline, the nation painfully remembers that God is who they must turn to for deliverance. And though their cries are in anguish, they are not to a useless idol but to the living God, maker of heaven and earth. For so long, they have pushed Him aside, but their discipline will draw them near once again. The author of Hebrews speaks to this truth in Hebrews 12:11 when he says, "No discipline seems enjoyable at the time, but painful. Later on, however, it yields the peaceful fruit of righteousness to those who have been trained by it." Israel's discipline, through the fall of Jerusalem, is painful, and their exile would last for seventy years, but it would yield righteousness through the faithful furtherance of God's plan of redemption.

Reading about the fall of Jerusalem should lead us to hope and not despair. And though that might seem hard in light of all they faced, we know from Scripture that God was at work in redemptive history through His people. Though they faced discipline, a remnant would return to Jerusalem one day, a remnant through which the Messiah would come.

God's discipline of Israel should remind us of two truths—the seriousness of our sin and the graciousness of our God. We are just as rebellious and disobedient as the Israelites. Our sin deserves God's wrath, but in His love and compassion, He sent His Son to take our place. And just as the Israelites cried out to God, knowing that He was the only One who would hear them, we cry out to the only One who provides salvation—Jesus.

HOW DOES THE ACCOUNT OF JERUSALEM'S FALL IN JEREMIAH 52 AND LAMENTATIONS 1:10–11 FULFILL THE CURSES FOUND IN DEUTERONOMY 28? WHAT DOES THIS TEACH US ABOUT GOD'S SOVEREIGNTY?

WHAT ARE THE TWO TRUTHS WE CAN LEARN FROM ISRAEL'S DISCIPLINE? HOW DOES THIS PROVIDE ENCOURAGEMENT FOR YOU AS YOU CONTINUE YOUR STUDY OF LAMENTATIONS?

HOW HAVE YOU SEEN GOD'S DISCIPLINE IN YOUR LIFE LEAD TO THE FRUIT OF RIGHTEOUSNESS?

SIN AGAINST A HOLY GOD IS COSTLY, WHICH IS WHY JESUS'S DEATH WAS SO NECESSARY FOR SALVATION.

MY EYES, MY EYES
Read Lamentations 1:12–16

This long quotation from the mouth of Lady Jerusalem herself summarizes much of what we have heard about the cause for her grief. With her own lips she now recounts her condition and her incomparable pain.

After crying out to the Lord, Jerusalem turns to anyone who will listen, even calling out to people who pass by in the streets, pleading with them to hear and have compassion on her. One of the hardest things about grief is the sense of loneliness that can accompany it, worsened only by a reality of actually being alone, as is the case for Jerusalem. She is drowning in the very independence she had fought so hard to achieve. Ironically, she reveals the conflict between her former desires and her present reality. Jerusalem had made the Lord her enemy, and now she is surprised to find that He is not on her side. While because of our union with Christ, we are never truly alone, we have all certainly felt as if we were alone in certain seasons and so can sympathize with Jerusalem in this sense.

She blames the Lord when describing what her enemies did. She does not speak of a plural attacker. Instead, it is He who has afflicted her—Yahweh. God promised to protect and care for Israel if they walked with and honored Him, but the people of Israel chose to rebel against the Lord. The Israelites forsook the Lord and His love and protection by serving false gods and by committing heinous acts of injustice within their city. In a harsh reversal of Psalm 18:16 when the Lord reaches down from on high to rescue, now the hand from on high does not come down to rescue Lady Jerusalem. She made her wishes clear to the Lord, and His response is the greatest cause for grief that a human can ever experience because He gave Jerusalem over to her desires.

Surely the events of the siege and exile were not what Jerusalem desired, her city set on fire, nets laid out on the ground to capture human lives, sickness due to hunger and grief spreading throughout the city. No, certainly not. We never want bad things to happen in our lives, even when we willfully sin. Her desire was for independence from the Lord and to be her own master. Even though God warned her profusely through the prophets what independence really meant, Jerusalem ignored His counsel. This devastation is what independence from the Lord meant. If not with Him, Jerusalem was against Him. Zephaniah 2:15 explains Jerusalem's rebellious mindset, as well as the result of her choices. Jerusalem did not just want independence, her people wanted to be a god to themselves.

This mindset is not much different than the one that Adam and Eve had in the garden when they first sinned. The serpent told them that if they disobeyed God's command, they would be made like God. They would be a god unto themselves and their own master. Sadly, Satan had fed them a lie, and the Israelites fed upon it in Jerusalem, even as our own modern world continues to do so today.

Jerusalem chose to serve something besides the Lord. Her transgressions had become her master, having their yoke upon her neck. A yoke is used to harness animals to get them to perform the tasks desired by their master. Jerusalem was enslaved to her own sin, bound by its commands as to a yoke. This enslavement made the people of Jerusalem weak and unable to fight when Babylon attacked. So, she was handed over to her enemies, and her people were literally yoked to one another and bound as slaves of Babylon.

When Jerusalem says that the Lord rejected her mighty men and warriors, this means that the city would face certain defeat. Israel knew that without the Lord on their side, the size of the army did not matter. The outcome of victory or defeat in battle was entirely in His hands. During times when their army was impossibly small, the Lord had given victory. God was Jerusalem's true "mighty man," but they had pushed Him away. Therefore, the result of their fight against Babylon is defeat and bloodshed.

Personified Jerusalem expresses defensiveness and regret. In Hebrew, the line in verse 16 that speaks of her weeping repeats, "my eyes," for emphasis. Like the uncontrollable sobs of a little child, she cries out, exhausted from weeping so often. She weeps knowing that the Lord was the one behind her suffering. The Babylonians were the ones who set fires, laid nets, bound yokes, and carried off the Israelites as prisoners, but Lady Jerusalem uses the singular pronoun, *he*, to speak about her pursuer. The Lord is now in the position of an enemy from her perspective. She cannot see Him chastening her. She can only see the guilt of her sin and the desolation it caused as the Lord reveals His wrath against her. Israel's sovereign, holy God acted justly in response to their sin but not in order to destroy them. God had not left Jerusalem forever. He would eventually rescue her from herself as He has continually done for His people throughout history.

Sin against a holy God is costly, which is why Jesus's death was so necessary for salvation. On our own, we are incapable of getting rid of our sin. In Ephesians 2:1, Paul says that we are dead in our sins. Just like Jerusalem, without the Lord we would be forever enslaved to sin as our master. God sent Jesus to remove the yoke of sin that was tied around our neck, and Jesus placed it on His neck on the cross. Because Jesus conquered sin, it has no power over us. Jesus dealt with it fully and finally so that when we confess it and trust in Him, we are saved from slavery to the enemy we once pursued.

We may still struggle with wanting control over more areas of life, but we can surrender that desire to the Lord's better, sovereign hand. Sin does not have any power over us unless we allow it. It is good to confess our sins daily to the Lord, not because it earns us forgiveness but because it reminds us of our ultimate dependence upon Jesus.

READ PSALM 127:1, 1 SAMUEL 2:7, AND COLOSSIANS 1:16–17. IS ANYONE EVER REALLY INDEPENDENT FROM GOD? WHY OR WHY NOT?

WHY IS GOD'S WRATH TOWARD JERUSALEM AN EXAMPLE OF JUSTICE, AND HOW CAN WE TAKE COMFORT IN THE FACT THAT GOD IS JUST TOWARD SIN?

HOW CAN WE TAKE COMFORT IN THE FACT THAT GOD IS MERCIFUL TOWARD SINNERS?

READ ROMANS 6:1–14. HOW CAN WE RESPOND TO OUR SIN BECAUSE OF WHAT CHRIST HAS DONE? WRITE A PRAYER, BRINGING YOUR SIN BEFORE THE LORD AND ASKING HIM TO SHOW YOU HOW TO LOVE HIM MORE THAN THOSE THINGS.

GOD DID
NOT PUNISH
JERUSALEM'S
SIN AND IGNORE
OURS. JESUS
DEALT WITH
BOTH.

HOMESICK WANDERERS

Read Lamentations 1:17

The poet interrupts the grieving Lady Jerusalem to describe her appearance as she mourns. The poet refers to her as Zion in this verse. Zion is described as reaching out her hands like a beggar or a little baby. The city is seeking comfort and security, but there is no one to answer the call. This is the fourth time we hear that Lady Jerusalem is comfortless. Isaiah 1:15 reminds us that the Lord had warned her of this fate if she continued in rebellion. Her hands and streets, bloodied by sin, are the reason the Lord hides His face from her.

When the poet speaks about Jerusalem as Jacob, it is a reminder of God's covenant with His people. God had renewed this covenant many years before during Jacob's life (Genesis 27). But here, God's command does not seem to be for Jacob; it is against him. Even the neighboring cities look on the impurity of Jerusalem and turn away from her. They do not attempt to help her because the Lord had decreed judgment on Jerusalem specifically. The other nations were sinful too, but God had not made a covenant with them.

Jerusalem's sin is so great that even among other nations, she is the impure one. In a way, she has become like her neighbors because she is now without the Lord's favor. In another way, she is now worse than the other nations by the depth of her sin. Her people have been cast out of the city, and those left behind are suffering greatly under oppression. Isaiah 1:4 explains her condition as estrangement from the Lord. The image of Lady Jerusalem extending her hands like an infant reaching for its mother or father is tender. It sadly reminds us of the very orphans and widows that the people of Jerusalem trampled and ignored in their rebellion and injustice (Isaiah 1:23). God is a God of justice, and Jerusalem had done many wrongs that the Lord was now seeking to make right.

Because of their impurity, Jerusalem's temple was destroyed. God had designed the temple as the place for cleansing sin. Today we do not need to go to a temple and offer sacrifices in order to be cleansed from our sins by a priest. Jesus is our Great High Priest in heaven, and He made a full and final sacrifice for all of our sins on the cross (Hebrews 4:14–16). But in the Old Testament, God made a way for His people to be cleansed from sins through provisional sacrifices, until Jesus came. This way, God could dwell with His people even then.

The temple was also God's dwelling place among them. The fact that Jerusalem bears the name Zion meant that God heard and answered her in distress. Now Zion feels her need for the Lord's presence more than ever, but she has chosen punishment by her rebellion, and so He has departed from her midst. She is estranged from the Lord just like Isaiah prophesied. In Jeremiah 4:31, Jeremiah describes Zion stretching out her hands in so much pain that he likens her to a woman giving birth for the very first time. The Lord has cast her off, and the pain of His absence is unbearable. But He will not cast her out forever.

God was still caring for Jerusalem and all her people, even as He chastened her for sins. The fact that the Lord disciplined Jerusalem is proof that He truly cared for her. In the same way that parents discipline their child in order to teach, train, and keep them safe from future harm, the Lord disciplines His children. It is important to remember God's character as we read Lamentations. It may be confusing that the Lord seems so harsh to them in their pain. It may cause us to wonder if the Lord is harsh with or far from you when you sin, like Jerusalem. But the truth is that God's punishment of His people in Lamentations was His response to great injustice that

they had done against other people. God had compassion on those other people — the widows and orphans whom the Israelites had ignored or harmed, the children they had trampled, and the weak whom they had abused. So God responded justly to Israel's injustices, and soon He would respond to the injustice done against them during the siege and exile.

Even though Jerusalem ran from the Lord and into this mess, He would rescue her anyway. One day He would show her a truly comfortless one when Jesus died on the cross. When Jesus hung on the tree, His arms were stretched out too but in a different way. Lady Jerusalem's hands were stretched out because of her own sin and the suffering that it brought. Jesus's hands were not stretched out for His own sins because He did not have any. His arms were extended for her sins and yours. Jesus laid down His life so that your life would never be truly taken from you. Jesus carried your sin to the grave so that even when you run toward it, it cannot own you. Jesus is God's answer to Jerusalem's plea.

Jesus did not do any of this to make the Father love you. God has always loved you, and that is why He sent Jesus to die. His death brought you near to God so that you would never again have to be estranged from Him. God did not punish Jerusalem's sin and ignore ours. Jesus dealt with both. He gave the straining child's hands access to the Father and His eternal comfort. You have that access today. You can talk to the Lord anywhere, at any time, and He will hear you because of Christ. Even if you are prone to wander like Jerusalem, His loving hold on you is firm.

WHAT CAN YOU LEARN ABOUT GOD'S CHARACTER FROM THIS PASSAGE?

HOW CAN YOU TAKE COMFORT TODAY IN THE KNOWLEDGE THAT GOD WILL ONE DAY RIGHT ALL WRONGS AND BRING PERFECT JUSTICE TO THE WORLD?

WHEN YOU ARE STRUGGLING WITH SIN, IN THAT MOMENT, HOW DO YOU FEEL LIKE THE LORD SEES YOU?

READ ROMANS 8:1 AND HEBREWS 12:3-11. HOW DOES THE SCRIPTURE SAY THAT HE SEES YOU?

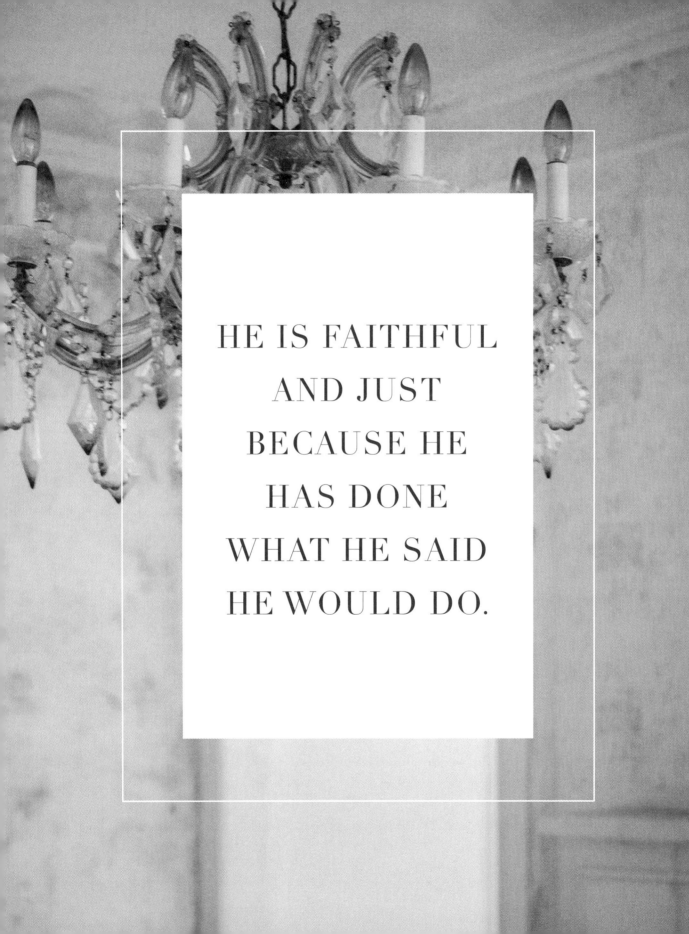

HE IS FAITHFUL
AND JUST
BECAUSE HE
HAS DONE
WHAT HE SAID
HE WOULD DO.

THE LORD IS RIGHTEOUS

Read Lamentations 1:18–19 and Nehemiah 9:26–37

The poet has certainly explained the reason for Jerusalem's suffering in previous verses, but for the first time we hear an acknowledgement of guilt from Lady Jerusalem's own lips. The Lord is righteous because she has rejected His good word. Though she will continually waver between remorse and self-pity, for at least this brief moment in the book, Lady Jerusalem sees herself clearly and the Lord rightly; the Lord is righteous in His actions toward her. He is faithful and just because He has done what he said He would do.

Years later, in the book of Nehemiah, the prophet humbly confesses the depth of Israel's sins against the Lord. He also expresses his firm belief in God's righteousness and mercy toward them, before and during the time of exile. Nehemiah recognizes that the Lord was far from punishing Israel the way that they truly deserved.

Lady Jerusalem seems to be warning those who listen about the consequences of rejecting the Lord's words. With Him, they found peace and provision. Apart from Him, there has been only tragedy and exile. Why had they ever doubted His love? Lady Zion describes the exile again, which consisted primarily of the young, healthy members of the city being taken into captivity while the older and weaker ones were left behind and oppressed within their own city. The result of spurning the Lord and His words has meant hunger, sickness, and death; this was because food, health, and life all flowed from the hands of the God whom she had rejected. This has led to the destruction of her walls and temple and the loss of the Lord's presence in her midst.

The warning continues as Jerusalem relays the strategies that she used to attempt her own deliverance. She called out to her lovers but found that they were traitors. Next, she addresses the priests and the elders. The priests would have been the ones who could carry out confession of sin, which meant admitting what she had done, and then they would cleanse her in the temple. The elders should have directed her to seek the Lord and obey His words before all of this took place. Instead, the temple has been destroyed, and the priests and elders wander the streets just as she does. They are looking for food in order to keep themselves alive; how could they help her now?

Lady Jerusalem begins the process of repentance in verse 18, and it is a glimmer of hope that the Lord is not far from her. Repentance happens when we see our sin and then turn away from it toward the Lord. It is a gift from God, so it cannot be conjured up by our own will power. The Lord is clearly tugging at Jerusalem's heart and gently calling her back to Himself. This posture of confession is the best place for Jerusalem to be.

God tells us in Psalm 51 that He will not despise a humble heart that knows and grieves its own sin. Psalm 51 is a beautiful example of confession. It is King David's prayer to the Lord after sinning by committing murder and adultery. As Jerusalem also meditates on her sin against the Lord and does not try to hide it with self-pity, she will demonstrate humility.

If Jerusalem had heeded the words of the Lord, it would never have deceived her like her false lovers had. Following the Lord's instruction would never have left her people hungry or stranded. Heeding His words would never have resulted in the mistreatment of her orphans and widows. The reference to His command probably refers to the law that God had given His people to live by, as Nehemiah explained. But throughout the New Testament, Jesus is also often referred to as the Word of God. The Greek is λογος, which literally means word. Jesus is the incarnate Word of God, and He is a true groom who had no deceit on His tongue (1 Peter 2:22). He fed many during His earthly ministry, and through the Bible, God continues to feed people by the word of the gospel.

One of the greatest gifts of Jesus's work is that He granted us eternal access to the Father, to whom we can confess our sins directly. We do not confess our sins in order to earn righteousness or cleanse ourselves. All of our sins, past, present, and future, were paid for by Jesus on the cross. But we get to come to the throne room of God daily through prayer and confess our sins there, not so that we can gain righteousness but because Jesus is already righteous in our place. We confess our sins with full assurance that God the Father hears us and sees Jesus's perfection instead of our sin. He gives us repentance and a clean conscience.

We confess our need for the blood of Christ to daily cover us. Our sin should sober us like it sobered Jerusalem. But then we must let the Lord's kindness lead us to repentance and accept the righteousness of Christ in our place. Jerusalem's primary mistake was refusing to rest in the gifts God had lavished on her. As we fight against the same temptation, we must remember that the work that Christ has done is enough for us, even though our own never will be. Then, we can strive and stumble toward reflecting Him, joyfully living in God's daily grace for us.

All of our sins, past, present, and future, were paid for by Jesus on the cross.

ARE THERE SINS IN YOUR OWN LIFE THAT YOU NEED TO CONFESS TODAY? SPEND SOME TIME IN PRAYER, ACKNOWLEDGING YOUR SIN BEFORE THE LORD AND MEDITATING ON HIS GIFT OF GRACE TO YOU.

READ ROMANS 5:1–11. WRITE DOWN ALL OF THE BLESSINGS THAT THOSE WHO KNOW JESUS RECEIVE IN THIS PASSAGE.

WHAT DO THE PASSAGES FROM TODAY REVEAL ABOUT GOD'S CHARACTER?

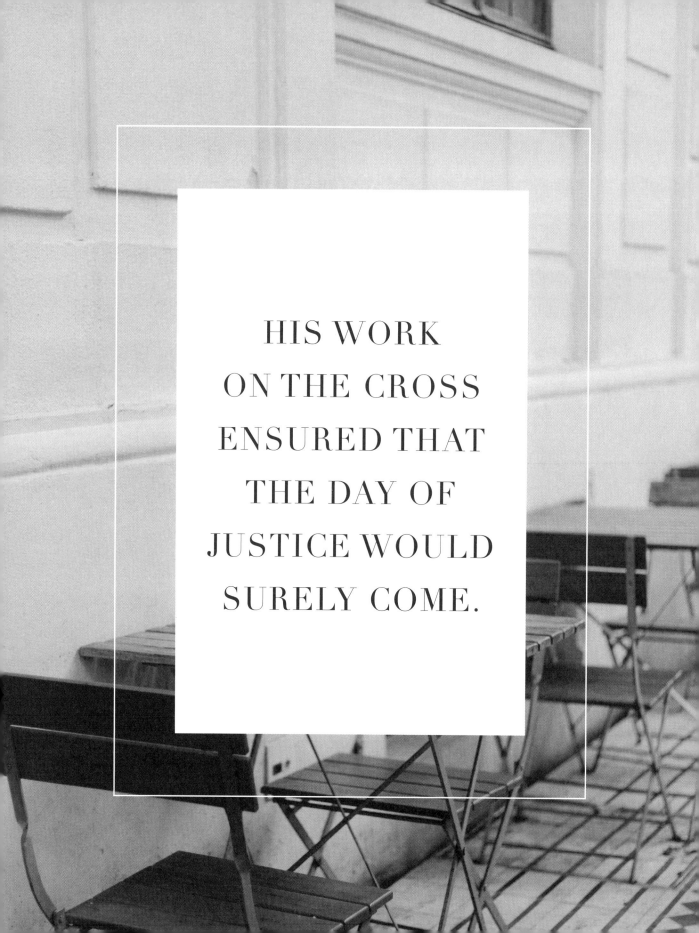

HIS WORK
ON THE CROSS
ENSURED THAT
THE DAY OF
JUSTICE WOULD
SURELY COME.

THE DAY OF THE LORD: INSIDE AND OUTSIDE THE GATE
Read Lamentations 1:20–22 and Nehemiah 9:32–37

Lady Jerusalem turns her call once again to the Lord. This passage is possibly the most humble speech from her lips. She is wracked with anxiety and goes on to describe the symptoms of it: distress, a churning stomach, and a troubled heart. These symptoms of anxiety are not foreign to us either. But the woman acknowledges that her present condition and the state of her heart are direct results of her rebellion against the Lord. There is great strife, both inside and outside the city. For the fifth time she mourns that there is no one to comfort her. The surrounding nations can clearly see her distress, and yet they look on and rejoice at her downfall.

The woman speaks about the day that the Lord has announced in the past against her enemies. This day of the Lord is spoken of in detail in Moses' song in Deuteronomy 32 when he speaks about the waywardness of Israel but also about God's jealousy for His name and His people. God will one day defeat Israel's enemies in His wrath against their injustice. Moses and now Jerusalem both want the Lord to swiftly bring this day.

Up to this point in the passage, the author has spoken as if the day of the Lord had come against Jerusalem instead of against her enemies. This is not true, but the magnitude of her suffering has muddied her memory. In a moment of clarity, Lady Jerusalem remembers the Lord's promise to her and His character. She acknowledges that His punishment of her has been more than just, but now these godless people are taking credit for His victory. Her plea is that God would be fair in administering justice against her enemies for their wickedness just as He rightfully dealt with her own.

In Nehemiah, the prophet continues his own prayer which mirrors the cries of Lady Jerusalem. He testifies to the Lord's righteousness and justice in punishing them for their unfaithfulness. Then he asks that God would look on the injustice now being done against His people at the hands of their Babylonian enemies, to whom the Lord had given them over. The prophet asks that the Lord would hasten the day He promised—the day when He would destroy all their adversaries.

While the request of both the woman and the prophet are unsettling to read, we can understand their pleas. In fact, their call for punishment to come on the nations who had harmed them is pleasing to the Lord's ears. It means they are asking for the very thing that God promised. It means they recognize His justice. It means that they are jealous for His name. Jerusalem is not complaining that she has been punished. She is calling out for her enemies to be judged for their unjust behavior just as she has been punished for hers.

In Moses' song in Deuteronomy, he explains that their enemies could never prevail against God's people unless the Lord allowed them. It is written, "But their 'rock' is not like our Rock" (Deuteronomy 32:31). Israel's enemies are by themselves. They have no chance of ultimate victory. We often deal with earthly enemies in daily life, such as those who want to harm us, sin that easily entraps, or people who distort or deny the gospel. When we face anxiety because we feel threatened by things in the world that are not of the Lord, we can ask God to bring the day that He promised; our prayers will sound different than those of Lady Zion, but our ultimate desire is the same as theirs: healing and peace.

The final day of the Lord has not come yet, but it was initiated by Jesus's death and resurrection. His work on the cross ensured that the day of justice would surely come and that all God's enemies—all our enemies—would be crushed under Jesus's feet. God promised this day of justice for the very first time in Genesis 3:15. He promised that the offspring of the woman would crush the head of the serpent and by doing so would defeat all His enemies. Jesus is the offspring, and He has defeated the devil and taken death's sting away (1 Corinthians 15:55). One day, on that righteous day of the Lord, He will make all things right.

The anxiety that overwhelmed Lady Jerusalem because of her sin and other earthly enemies is not an unfamiliar feeling to any of us. While it is comforting to cling to the promise of the coming day of justice, there are also promises about today. Sometimes the anxious feelings we experience are because of our own sin, and the Lord grieves with us in that. And sometimes they are just the fruit of living in a world where injustice is rampant, and daily life reminds us of it. If your heart is gripped with anxiety today, find comfort in Jesus's strength that is greater than your own. Call out to the Lord in prayer, read His Word, and meditate on it when anxious thoughts come. You may not be free from anxiety until heaven, but the Lord will never leave you alone in it. He is a warrior on your behalf, and His victory is already secure. You are hidden in Him, and no amount of sin, inside or outside of you, can shake that firm foundation.

Find comfort in Jesus's strength that is greater than your own.

READ REVELATION 21:1–8.
WHAT BLESSINGS WILL THERE BE IN
THE NEW HEAVEN AND THE NEW EARTH?

LIST ALL THE ACTIONS AND QUALITIES
OF GOD THAT NEHEMIAH MENTIONS IN
TODAY'S PASSAGE.

READ PSALM 73:26. HOW DOES THIS VERSE GIVE COMFORT TO DISTRESSED
OR ANXIOUS HEARTS?

LAMENTATIONS 3:20

I continually remember them and have become depressed.

Week Two Reflection

REVIEW LAMENTATIONS 1:10–22

Paraphrase the passage from this week.

What did you observe from this week's text about God and His character?

What does this week's passage reveal about the condition of mankind and about yourself?

_____

_____

_____

_____

How does this passage point to the gospel?

_____

_____

_____

_____

_____

How should you respond to this passage? What is the personal application?

_____

_____

_____

_____

What specific action steps can you take this week to apply this passage?

_____

_____

_____

_____

_____

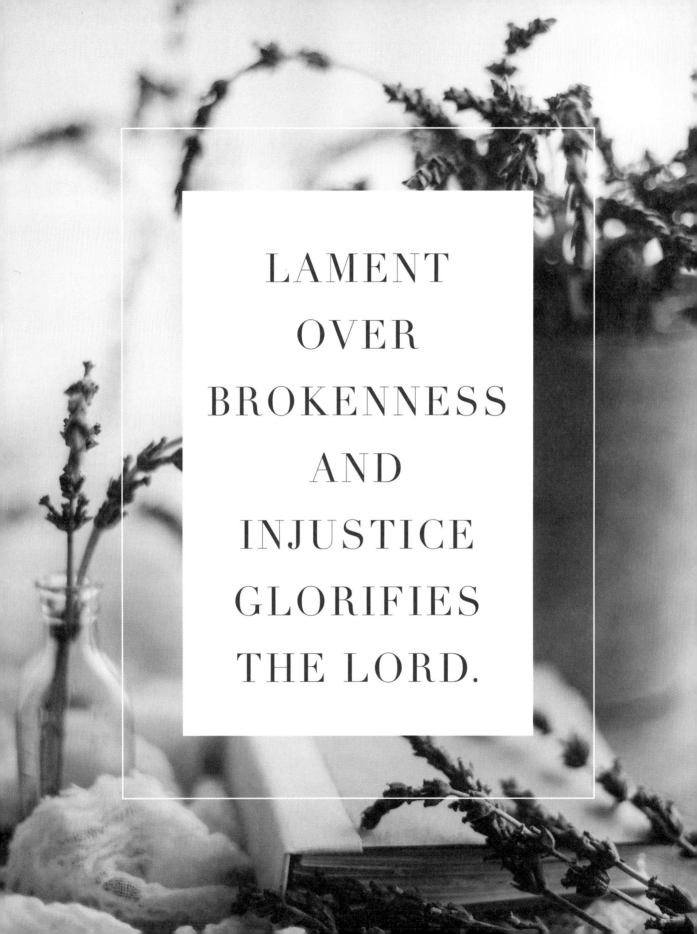

LAMENT OVER BROKENNESS AND INJUSTICE GLORIFIES THE LORD.

WHERE JUSTICE AND MERCY MEET

Read Lamentations 2:1–5 and Isaiah 1:21–26

The second poem begins with the same exclamatory word that opened the book. The poet expresses surprise and grief at how the Lord's anger has attacked His own people. As the writer goes on to describe God's anger in the first half of this poem, we begin to hear his own anger too. He mentions Israel's glory being thrown down from heaven to earth, which probably refers to the temple — God's dwelling place among His chosen people — being struck down and destroyed. As the poet acknowledges in a few verses, God has made Himself like an enemy toward Jerusalem.

Verse 2 can be challenging to read with the stark words, "no compassion," or "without mercy," in some translations. As the poet looks around at the homes of the offspring of Jacob, one whom God promised to bless and to prosper his descendants, it appears to him that the Lord has forgotten His own promises. The poet sees how God has destroyed the city of Judah, and he uses the familial language of daughter to attempt to describe how intimate the damage feels — God has let loose His anger on His own people, His own daughter.

The horns of Israel may refer to their power and confidence but also to the altar in the temple which would have been adorned with horns used for consecration — making things holy. The Lord had cut off the city's might and their means of cleansing. God's right hand, the same one that defended and delivered the Israelites from their Egyptian captors, was now turned against them. The poet describes God's anger like a consuming fire. This powerful quality of God that is praised and reverenced by those in His protection is the greatest fear of those who have set themselves against Him (Hebrews 12:28–29).

The bow that the Lord has strung is Babylon, He wields as a weapon. The cup of God's wrath has been filling for centuries, while Jerusalem failed to heed the warnings He gave them through the prophets. Now, it is being poured out onto Daughter Zion.

The wickedness of Israel's sin had grown past the time for warning mercies. But the people did not believe that God meant what He had warned in the covenant. God is angry now, and He does not shy away from stating that fact very clearly throughout this book. God's anger is not like our human anger. We cannot fully comprehend what the Scriptures mean when they talk about God having emotions because His emotions are without sin. His emotions are always pure. But He uses human language in the Bible to describe something un-human that is taking place within the Godhead. The human analogy to that true reality, in this case, is anger.

For the second time in this chapter, the poet calls God an enemy in verse 5. It is tempting to skim this description and chalk it up to name calling from the mouth of an angry and hurting poet. But there is truth in it. The Lord is in the position of an enemy toward His people during this time in Israel's history. He had mercifully cautioned them that if they did not repent, this alienation would be the consequence. His people had become murderers, rapists, temple-defilers, thieves, and abusers (Isaiah 1:21–23). In reality, Jerusalem had been behaving like an enemy to God for years, yet He had cared for her. But now, the day that the Lord long announced had arrived. He would bring justice upon their injustice.

In Isaiah 1:21–26, there is an unfaithful city that God restored by a refining process. The process was painful and meant destruction of the old, sinful ways. It meant that things tainted by sin had to be stripped and rebuilt. But the result of this refining would be a righteous and faithful city. This passage was God's covenant plan for Jerusalem. He would refine and restore her to Himself. God's warning mercies had come to an end when Babylon invaded, but His nature as merciful never ceased because God does not change (Malachi 3:6). Jerusalem deserved to be wiped out because of their sinful actions. By His mercy God did not utterly destroy them, but in His justice, He dealt with their sin.

God did not ignore Israel's sin or leave them in it, and the same is true for all of those who trust in Christ. Israel's story is our history. We were once enemies of God, dead in our transgressions (Ephesians 2:1). God could have ignored our sin, but that would not have been just. He could have left us to sin ourselves to death and face eternal punishment, but it is because of the Lord's great mercy that we have not been consumed by His holy wrath. The cross is where God's justice and mercy meet. Jesus was the only one who could face the wrath of God without being consumed. And He did.

He did so because even as the poet cries out in angry tears at the Lord, God is weeping right along with him over the destruction that sin has caused. God and the poet both see the wickedness that Israel is now experiencing from the Babylonians, and they lament. Lament over brokenness and injustice glorifies the Lord. God models lament for us all throughout Scripture as He grieves over His wayward people. It is because of God's anger and sadness over sin that we have a Savior. We were once far off from God because our sin deserved His wrath, but we have now been brought near to Him by the blood of Jesus, God's own Son (Ephesians 2:13).

But there is still much to lament because of the damage that sin continues to do. We must learn to lament over these things like Jesus and then act justly while loving mercy as He does.

HOW IS IT COMFORTING TO KNOW THAT GOD NEVER CHANGES?

HOW DOES THE PATTERN OF SINFULNESS, REFINING, AND RESTORATION FOUND IN ISAIAH 1 APPLY TO THE LIFE OF EVERY CHRISTIAN?

WHY IS ANGER, RIGHTLY USED, A NECESSARY EMOTION IN RELATION TO SIN?

WE CAN
NEVER LIVE
UP TO GOD'S
STANDARD.
WE WILL
ALWAYS NEED
ATONEMENT.

NO WORSHIP, NO WALL, NO WORD

Read Lamentations 2:6–10

The poet provides a specific list of the most valuable things that Jerusalem has lost: God has destroyed His temple, He has torn down the city walls, and He has ceased to give counsel through earthly advisors. The poet rightly blames God as the one who removed these gifts from His people.

The temple, in addition to the place of sacrifice and cleansing for sin, was also where they celebrated festivals like Passover, the Feast of Booths, the Day of Atonement, and every Sabbath—worship festivals for praising God for the ways He had rescued, provided, and cared for Israel. Festivals were a central tradition in temple worship, a mandate from God, and a time for jubilee. Now, instead of jubilant songs of praise from God's people, the temple was filled with the harsh cries of enemies who were tearing it down. Rather than joyfully worshiping, the people are mourning on the ground, grieving the dead and lost among them. The women of Jerusalem prostrate on the floor is likely symbolic of fallen soldier-husbands and sick, dying children. In refusing to worship the Lord and partake of temple blessings, the Lord removed these gifts from Israel.

Verse 6 also speaks of the kings and priests who were responsible for modeling repentance and worship for the people. Instead, they had fed them lies and fostered corruption. They thought that surely God would not destroy His own temple, and they were certain that the building itself meant defense from attackers. But Solomon, when he built the temple, was very clear that God was not bound by or to the temple building itself (1 Kings 8:27). Now God's presence was far from it, and the punishment of the city leaders is severe. King Zedekiah, the ruler of Israel during the siege, was captured. He watched his family murdered before his eyes, removing the possibility of descendants. His eyes were then cut out, and he likely died soon after, in a prison cell (Jeremiah 52:1–11). This moment in Israel's history is grave because they cannot see hope for another king. Had God's promise to preserve Israel been broken? If there was no king, who would carry on the line of David that was supposed to lead all the way to the Messiah?

In 587 BC, the city walls were destroyed as verse 8 recounts. The protective wall around Daughter Zion is gone. Her insides are laid bare and vulnerable to attack. God had planned this destruction. The measuring line in verse 8 was a tool used for careful planning, which reveals that God's actions were premeditated. It was not the result of impulse or sudden fury but years of Israel's failure to heed God's merciful warnings. Jerusalem's physical condition now outwardly reflects her spiritual state.

Zion's kings, leaders, and teachers are among the nations in exile. They are no longer present to teach the people what God has said through the prophets, and the prophets themselves receive no new word from God. They pleaded to be like the nations, so God tore down the wall that separated them from the surrounding peoples. After they stopped their ears to His voice, the Lord removed His words from the mouths of the leaders and prophets. God appears to be silent. Had He disowned them?

Jerusalem desperately needed to be cleansed and to worship, to be defended, and to hear from the Lord. But there was no longer a temple for worship, no wall for protection, and no word from the Lord. These needs were not new, and they are the same needs we have always had as creatures of God. But in order to praise Him rightly, someone must pay for our sin. On our own, we cannot approach God's throne room in any earthly temple, or in any heavenly one, because we are dirtied by sin. We owe our Creator obedience and honor as His creatures, but we have been rebellious and sinful against Him

instead. That sin has to be atoned for so that we can be reconciled to God to restore the relationship. Atonement means righting a wrong that was done against someone, like the payment of a debt. It cleanses from sin and makes us pure before the Lord.

The reality is that we can never live up to God's standard. We will always need atonement because we sin more and more every day that we have breath in our lungs. And no animal sacrifice can ever fully pay that debt. Just like the Israelites in the Old Testament, we have failed to meet God's covenant standards. That is why God fulfilled the covenant Himself, through Jesus. Jesus not only met every stipulation of the covenant perfectly, but He also laid down His life on God's altar as a sufficient act of atonement for our sin (1 John 2:2). He is why we no longer need to sacrifice in a temple in order to worship God rightly. He is our protection because He conquered our enemies by His death. And He is God's full and final word to us.

Jerusalem could not make atonement in the temple at this time, but God considered Jesus's coming sacrifice of Himself as sufficient for even the past. His people did not have to demonstrate righteousness, they just needed faith in the One who is righteous (Romans 3:22). In the same way, when you accept Jesus as your Savior, not only are your present and future sins covered, but even the sins of your past are paid for by His precious blood. And in this news, jubilee is restored.

Jerusalem wondered who would carry on David's kingly line after Zedekiah's death. They wondered who the Messiah would be that the prophets spoke of — the one who would bring salvation to the people of God. Jesus was always God's plan for our redemption, and He would see that to completion.

READ MATTHEW 1 TO SEE A PREVIEW OF HOW GOD REMAINED FAITHFUL TO THE DAVIDIC LINE, EVEN THROUGH THE BABYLONIAN EXILE.

WHAT DOES THIS PASSAGE REVEAL ABOUT GOD'S CHARACTER?

HOW IS IT COMFORTING TO KNOW THAT JESUS HAS FULLY PAID FOR ALL YOUR SINS, PAST, PRESENT, AND FUTURE?

GOD IS JUST,
AND HE CARES
FOR THE
OPPRESSED
AND VICTIMS
OF INJUSTICE.

A GLORIOUS TENSION

Read Lamentations 2:11–13 and Jeremiah 30:12–17

Now the poet voices his own grief for Daughter Zion. He has been weeping over her with such intensity that he feels as though his heart has come up out of his chest. This may mean that he is experiencing physical sickness because of the severity of his sorrow. His reaction is not surprising. Even children are fainting in the streets, feeble from hunger. They turn to their mothers and cry out to be fed like a nursing infant. Weak from starvation, they are compared to a man wounded in battle.

The poet repeats, "the streets of the city," in these verses, possibly to signify how public this scene of mother and child is. There is nowhere to grieve privately. Jerusalem's shame and sorrow are laid bare. Literally, there are no walls to shut the city off from view anymore. The children are mentioned again in verse 12, described like nursing infants at their mothers' breast. But instead of the nourishment and sustenance they should find there, the babies die on their mother's chest. This scene is a perversion of God's design, and the little ones suffer for the sins of their parents.

In verse 13, the poet speaks directly to personified Jerusalem for the first time. The woman pleaded in chapter 1 for someone to see her suffering and show pity, so the poet now tries to answer this request. But just looking at her destruction makes him sick. How can he defend her, knowing the depth of her sin? The poet tries to comfort her, but he cannot even fathom a scenario similar to what she has experienced. Her cause for grief is like no other, so he cannot even imagine what a favorable outcome might look like. Is one even possible?

We have to remember that the Lord is the author of Lamentations, grieving along with the poet. We can see the reality of this as we look at other Scriptures such as Jeremiah 30:12–17. As you read Lamentations, especially 2:13, along with the Lord's speech in Jeremiah 30, the parallels to Lamentations are striking. Both passages speak of an incurable wound beyond comparison, deceitful lovers, a grief beyond comfort, a weighty guilt, and the Lord's hand in all of it. The stark difference between these two passages is that Jeremiah reveals the Lord's response to His people's grief in verses 16–17. The Lord has a plan for restoration. Just as He had planned for their deserved punishment, He had also ordained their salvation, even before He struck them (Ezekiel 34:11–12; Isaiah 12:3–4).

In Jeremiah 30, God reveals that He has indeed made Himself like an enemy, just as the poet accused Him. Both the poet and the Lord know that Jerusalem's suffering is the just result of her sins. And they both show compassion on this stricken woman. Even the Lord who has afflicted her mourns over her pain. How can this be? There will always be a conflict in our minds when we try to comprehend God's ways by using our own limited, emotional capacities. God is far more complex than we are—He is not like us. God does not rejoice over Jerusalem's downfall. Instead, through the prophets, He expresses grief that the harsh reality of her punishment was necessary because of the people's sin.

Now, Jerusalem is a weak and wallowing woman upon whom the Lord has tender mercy and compassion. He is not blind to her sin, but He has dealt with it. Psalm 12:5 says, "'Because of the devastation of the needy and the groaning of the poor, I will now rise up,' says the Lord. 'I will provide safety for the one who longs for it.'" And God did hear the neediness of Jerusalem and the groans of her whimpering, hungry babies. The Lord also looks on you with this same compassion. He saw you helpless in your sin, and He sees the pain that this sinful world continues to cause you. There is no need you have of which He is not aware and prepared to meet.

The complexity of justice and mercy that is found throughout Lamentations reflects the complexity of our God. The tension between justice and compassion is a common one in a world so afflicted by terrible sin but governed by a good God. The same tension can be found in Jesus's life and death, and He is the ultimate example of God's justice and mercy. It was by His great compassion for us that God sent Jesus, His only Son, to be stricken by our unjust sins in order to satisfy His divine justice against those very sins. As God, Jesus grieved for us in the deadness of our sinful condition. As God, He also knew that it deserved His wrath. In a marvelous symphony of wrath and compassion, justice and mercy, Father God struck Jesus the Son to punish sin and purchase redemption.

God never shies away from the truth. He never hides from the reality of sin in the life of His people. Even as He had compassion on Jerusalem in the aftermath of the affliction He had sent, He never ignored their guilt. It is mercy that He did not, because if God blinded Himself to sin, He never would have sent Jesus to rescue and redeem us from it.

Our modern world is still groaning under the weight of sin and its destructive consequences. The imagery of the hungry children in today's passage is a sadly familiar one to us. The world is still broken, and injustice is evident in every corner because of sin. But God is just, and He cares for the oppressed and victims of injustice (Psalm 9:9). We have to remember that with the same harmony of wrath and compassion, the Lord sees and knows, and He has planned from the beginning of the ages to make all things new, in His time. As we wait, we should pray on behalf of the oppressed and hurting and share the good news of Jesus with all.

WHAT DOES THIS PASSAGE REVEAL ABOUT GOD'S CHARACTER?

READ ROMANS 3:21–26. HOW DOES THE GOSPEL DEMONSTRATE BOTH GOD'S JUSTICE AND HIS COMPASSIONATE MERCY?

HOW CAN YOU PRAY FOR THE OPPRESSED AND VICTIMS OF INJUSTICE TODAY?

THE
WORLD
NEEDS A
SAVIOR.

WHO CAN HEAL?
Read Lamentations 2:14–17

Verse 13 ended with a genuine question from the poet: Who can heal Jerusalem's wounds? In the verses that follow, he attempts to reason out an answer. Could it be the prophets? The poet is not speaking about God's prophets here. He says, "your prophets." Before God sent this disaster on the city, He had given the people warning upon warning through His prophets such as Jeremiah and Isaiah. Instead, the people chose to listen to false prophets who prophesied lies and faulty promises of security. They refused to expose the iniquity—the sins—of the people. They tried to place a band-aid on a gushing wound. Jeremiah called out these false prophets, saying that they had told the people that there was peace when there really was no peace (Jeremiah 6:13–14). Hananiah was one false prophet who told these treacherous lies, and he died because he tried to lead God's people astray (Jeremiah 28). Clearly these liars are no help to Jerusalem now, either.

Next, the poet turns to Jerusalem's neighbors: Can they heal her? No, they only come near to mock and look on in astonishment at her downfall. This had been the city of Yahweh, and the neighboring towns evidently had once acknowledged her former beauty. Psalm 48:2 is the original description of Zion that the passersby now uses to taunt her. Jerusalem has fallen so far from the glory she had when the Lord was within her, and her neighbors offer no aid.

Her enemies are certainly no source of help, and in all their attacks, there is not even a hint of mercy or relent. Babylon hisses out words of violence against the Jerusalem woman, rejoicing at her fall because it is the day they have fought hard to see. Babylon mistakenly boasts that they have conquered the city entirely by themselves. In reality, the Lord wielded them as the mere weapon of His just wrath, and true victory belongs to Him alone. The enemies speak of the day that they have waited for, but we know that the true day of defeat has not yet come. On that day, God will destroy all of Israel's enemies (Zechariah 9:14–17).

Finally, the poet comes to the only shred of hope and help for Jerusalem. The Lord is the one who has done this to her. The only one powerful enough to heal this city is the One who wounded it. The Lord's decree was His covenant with Israel. In their rebellious disobedience, Jerusalem has invoked the curses of the covenant (Deuteronomy 28:45–50). The Lord has been nothing but faithful. This was not the first time that Israel had broken God's covenant, but God had been very patient with them and consistently warned them for centuries about the consequences of continued rebellion, all the while showing grace by delaying punishment. But the people did not want to face their sin.

Jerusalem's mistakes are uncomfortably familiar. There are many forms of false prophets in the world today, even in our daily lives. There are some who often go unperceived even by Christians. These prophets promise happiness and life apart from the living God. Sometimes their lies are in the form of self-help routines or life-changing products. They draw people into their deceit with the promises of money, sex, or fame. They call sin by different names in order to cover it up or glorify it. They speak peace when there is no peace.

Apostle Paul warns about people like this in Galatians 1:8. He says that there will be certain false teachers who come to preach a different gospel than the only true gospel of Jesus Christ. Paul says that these people may even come into the church and try to add or detract from the true message. They may refuse to call sin "sin" and tell people that there is no such thing. Or maybe they will tell people that they need works of the law in order to be justified, instead of the pure blood of Christ. Regardless of the lie they speak, these false teachers lead people astray, just like the false prophets in Jerusalem. The remedy for both enemies is the same: God's word must be our final source of truth. The message of Jesus Christ is God's final word to us. We have everything that we need to be saved in Christ, so we do not need another gospel.

The world needs a savior. Those who do not know Jesus are even more susceptible to the false prophets who encourage sin and even call it good, because they have no other hope to cling to. Every human knows that there is brokenness within them, and they try to fix it with anything and everything. Paul says that before someone becomes a Christian, that person has been suppressing the knowledge of his or her sinful condition and of God's existence (Romans 1:18). Maybe you are still in this place, too, trying to make yourself whole. Christ came to change your heart and open your eyes to your sin and to His offer of salvation. Have you accepted His offer and asked Him to be Lord of your life?

When you confess the reality of your sinfulness and accept Christ and His blood as the only form of salvation from that sin, you are saved. Your eyes are then open to your sin, and God gives you His Holy Spirit to live and work inside your heart. There is grief in this process because staring your sin in the face is a challenging necessity. But there is abundant joy in it as well, because you will receive the Holy Spirit who also reminds you of God's Word. He speaks the gospel to you, and you can instruct yourself in it by His Word, daily. It is there that you will daily find grace and hope for your sin and access to the only true healer.

WHAT ARE SOME EXAMPLES OF FALSE PROPHETS WHO TRY TO PRETEND THAT SIN IS NOT A REALITY IN THE WORLD TODAY?

READ 1 JOHN 4:1–12. WHY IS GOD'S OFFER OF SALVATION BETTER THAN THE PEACE THAT FALSE PROPHET'S PROMISE?

GOD DOES NOT PRETEND THAT YOUR BROKENNESS DOES NOT EXIST; HE HEALS IT. WHY SHOULD YOU NOT IGNORE SIN IN YOUR LIFE?

YAHWEH HAS
MADE HIMSELF
KNOWN AS
MERCIFUL AND
COMPASSIONATE.

A CRY OF HOPE
Read Lamentations 2:18–19

The poet has revealed that the Lord who afflicted Jerusalem is the only true hope for her deliverance. At the beginning of verse 18, there is mention of people who are already crying out to God. It is uncertain whether this is Jerusalem or others, but whoever it is, the poet pleads with Jerusalem to join in the lament.

He instructs even the broken walls of the city, also symbolic of all the inhabitants, to weep without ceasing before God. They are not to sleep or do anything but cry and lay their hearts bare before the Lord in prayer, day and night. Every day, they must take on this posture of humility. This posture can be seen elsewhere in Scripture. One example is in Psalm 51 again, which David wrote after he sinned by committing adultery with Bathsheba and murdering her husband. His guilt is heavy, and he can turn to no one but the Lord for healing and cleansing. In verse 17, David explains, "The sacrifice pleasing to God is a broken spirit. You will not despise a broken and humbled heart, God." This is what God wants from sinful people. The word "broken" in this passage is translated as contrite. The meaning is the same, but the word contrite offers some nuance that brokenness does not have.

To be contrite means to not only recognize your guilt but to experience remorse for the actions that made you guilty. Contrition is one of the humblest human experiences, and broken is a helpful synonym because it gives us a tangible picture of the contrite heart—it is broken and grieved over its own sin. The contrite heart desires to change and turn from its own sin but also recognizes that because it is broken, it is incapable of changing itself.

We see the elements of contrition in Lamentations. The poet gives the people of Jerusalem four commands: arise, cry out, pour out your heart, and lift up your hands. All of these actions are to be carried out before the Lord. It is to Him that they cry, it is before His presence that they pour out their hearts, and it is to Him that they lift their hands. The poet is calling them into a posture of humility and contrition.

They must present themselves before the Lord in all their brokenness and need, lifting empty hands up to the only fountain of supply. This is the only way they can approach the mighty God whom they have betrayed. If they will not do it for themselves, the poet pleads with them to do it for their children's sake.

Why would the poet tell Jerusalem to call out to the very One who has brought her pain? He has wounded her like this, so how can she even approach Him now? There are two realities at work here. The first is that the poet knows His God. Yahweh has made Himself known as merciful and compassionate, slow to anger and abounding in consistent and enduring love. The poet knows that God rescues the needy and takes on the cause of the oppressed (Psalm 12:5, 9:9). The second reality is that God is also the author of Lamentations. God, through the life and lungs of this human poet, instructs His people to lament their own sin and the sins that have been committed against them. He is calling them to do so before His presence, with humble and broken hearts. He wants them to drain their tears before Him and empty their lungs of grief in His presence, because He cares for them.

God does not delight in their pain; He laments over it. But God is glorified as they grieve the horrors that sin has caused. This lament acknowledges before God that things are not as they should be—the world is not operating the way that God originally designed. Lament also recognizes man's helplessness to fix the problem and confesses a need for God's redeeming and merciful grace to intervene. Lament is a form of hope—hope in what God will do one day to redeem and a longing for that reality.

Just like Jerusalem, as we lament sin before the Lord, we train our hearts to hate our sin and to crave God's mercy and perfection. We will also learn to grieve the sins of the world, which have caused the devastating brokenness in our world. Acknowledgement of our sin should always lead to confession and, by God's grace, repentance. As we deal with our own sin before the Lord, we can then come and ask Him for justice in the world around us, as we will see Jerusalem begin to do later on in the poem.

True lament ought to be a regular rhythm in the life of a Christian. A day never goes by when we have not sinned, so there will always be sin to grieve this side of heaven. Most days it will be mostly our own, but sometimes it will also be the sins of our family members, friends, nation, or world. The world is broken, and things are not as they should be. There is physical brokenness and more importantly, spiritual sickness. The hurting people in the world do not need a quick fix; they need the eternal God. And this God invites us to pour out our hearts to Him, promising to be a refuge for us (Psalm 62:8).

We need to enter into lament but not as those without hope. Grieving our sin in light of Christ means that we never have to mope or pout. We lament the reality of the fall and the pain and damage it has caused God's world, knowing that all will soon be restored in heaven. In our humble position of contrition, we must cling to what Christ accomplished on the cross to deal with all sin. Lament is a cry of hope, rooted in God's mercy and sovereignty, not a wallowing in despair. Why would we call out to Him unless we were confident in His plan and power to redeem? God invites us to lament what sin has broken in our world and to do so in confident peace because of Christ.

HOW HAVE YOU SEEN SIN DAMAGE GOD'S GOOD DESIGN FOR CREATION AND RELATIONSHIPS?

READ ISAIAH 41:17. HOW DOES GOD'S CHARACTER GIVE HOPE FOR JERUSALEM? HOW DOES IT GIVE YOU HOPE FOR YOUR OWN LIFE AND OUR WORLD?

READ JAMES 4:6–10. WHY IS HUMILITY AN IMPORTANT PART OF REPENTANCE FROM SIN?

LAMENTATIONS 3:21

Yet I call this to mind, and therefore I have hope

Week Three Reflection

Paraphrase the passage from this week.

_____

_____

_____

_____

_____

_____

_____

_____

_____

_____

_____

_____

_____

_____

_____

What did you observe from this week's text about God and His character?

_____

_____

_____

_____

_____

_____

_____

What does this week's passage reveal about the condition of mankind and about yourself?

_____

_____

_____

_____

How does this passage point to the gospel?

_____

_____

_____

_____

_____

How should you respond to this passage? What is the personal application?

_____

_____

_____

_____

What specific action steps can you take this week to apply this passage?

_____

_____

_____

_____

_____

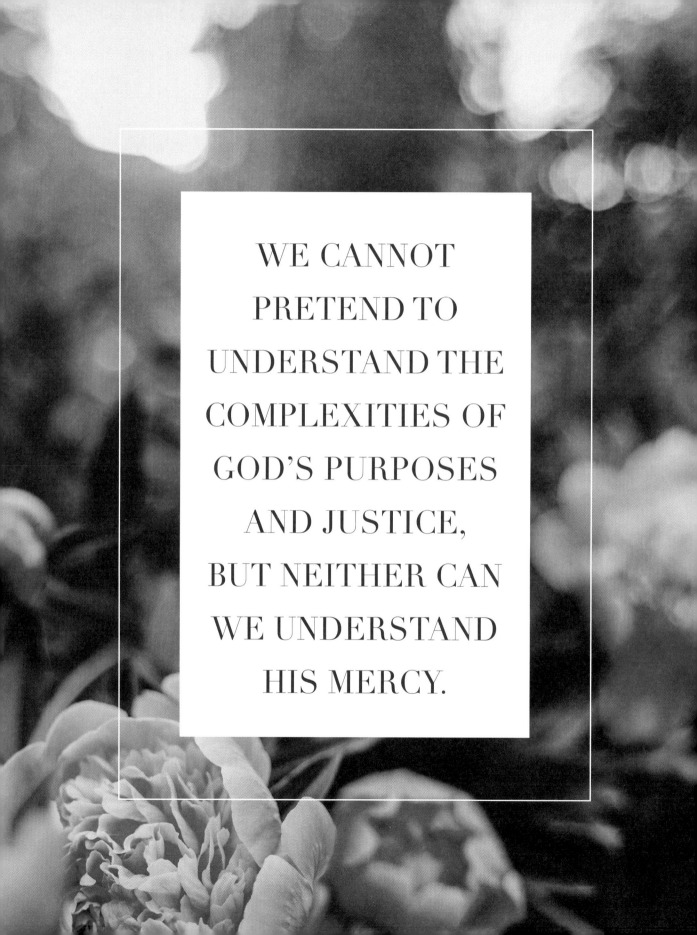

WE CANNOT
PRETEND TO
UNDERSTAND THE
COMPLEXITIES OF
GOD'S PURPOSES
AND JUSTICE,
BUT NEITHER CAN
WE UNDERSTAND
HIS MERCY.

QUESTIONS IN THE ANSWERS
Read Lamentations 2:20–22

The Jerusalem woman calls out to the Lord directly but not in the way that the poet requested. Rather than a posture of humility and repentance, the voice calls out, asking the Lord again to look and consider her condition. She does not ask for forgiveness or healing; she still has a case to make before the Lord. Several questions and a series of accusations follow. Jerusalem believes that God is punishing her excessively.

The first question asks God who else He has dealt with in this way. This question could be read as, "Who has ever received a punishment as bad as this from the Lord?" Or the question could refer to the covenantal identity of the Israelites. These are God's own people. How could He deal this way with His children? Does He not know whom He has afflicted? No, God knew exactly what He had done. It was precisely because of who they were that Israel faced these grim realities—they were God's covenant people.

The perversions of creation mentioned in the following questions are difficult to read. Mothers are eating their own children. Women who ought to be providing nourishment for their babies have made those babies their own food. This is a powerful perversion of God's good design and a symptom of starvation, devastatingly common in siege warfare. The reality of this picture is crushing to think of, and it should be. The blessings and curses of the covenant found in Deuteronomy 28, which we referenced earlier, were not to be lightly taken. In Deuteronomy 28:53, God warned Israel that this very cannibalism would result from their rebellion if they did not walk in the life of His good covenant (Deuteronomy 32:47).

The next perversion is that the priests and prophets are murdered in the temple. They were supposed to be holy people, set apart by God, but instead they have been slaughtered in the most holy place. Of course, these priests and prophets were not truly holy like they were called to be. These are the foolish priests and the false prophets who led the people astray. But Jerusalem can only see the temple, intended to be a place of protection, as a dangerous place now, where both priest and prophet have been killed.

The corruptions of nature continue into verse 21. Both old and young have returned to the dust in death. The young, who should have seen many years, have been cut down early. There is no one to bury them, so their bodies line the streets of ravaged Jerusalem. Both young men and young women have died by the sword in battle, cut off in their youth. Though the swords of Babylonian warriors accomplished this defeat, the Lord is the one who wielded them as the weapon of His wrath, and Jerusalem knows it.

Jerusalem accuses God of bringing this disaster on them. There are no survivors or escapees from this destruction—everyone has been killed or led off as captives. The children of her tender care and raising have been stripped from Jerusalem's motherly arms. She cannot yet bring herself to plead with the Lord for anything.

The people of Jerusalem had perverted the Lord's justice by their sin, and yet the consequences now appear unjust in their horror toward innocent children. But somehow, the punishment is still just toward the original ones who sinned. In many ways, we can ask similar questions alongside Jerusalem but not in anger or unrepentance. We may wrestle with why the Lord allowed Babylon not only to bring this dread on the Israelites but also why He was the one behind Babylon using them as a tool to carry out the horrors of this passage. Yet we know that even as Jerusalem tries to set up an antithesis here between her people and the Lord, these were God's own people, whose condition He too grieved over (Jeremiah 8:18–9:3).

The truth is that we do not fully understand God's dealings with His people, but we do know who He is. He is a God of His word. Jerusalem's punishment was not excessively harsh, and God's actions were not unjust. We cannot pretend to understand the complexities of God's purposes and justice, but neither can we understand His mercy.

The same questions about God's justice that we ask along with Jerusalem should fill our minds when we think of Christ. His death on the cross is a parallel to Jerusalem's suffering in many ways. Except this was God's own perfect Son. He had no sin and had done no injustice. He was nothing like wicked Jerusalem; He was God. And yet, God poured out His wrath on Jesus Christ, His Son whom He loved. This is the most unjust act of all. At least Jerusalem deserved punishment for their horrific sinfulness, but Jesus was sinless. Jesus's death was the most unjust death, because He did nothing to deserve the suffering and execution that He endured. But as God, Jesus satisfied true justice for our sins so that we would never experience it as fully as we deserved. What perfect justice and perfect mercy!

It is important to ask the Lord hard questions as we read His Word, but we do so humbly. We come to ponder and seek answers, asking the Holy Spirit to give us understanding where the Scriptures reveal it. God is all-knowing and supremely good; we are not. We cannot even understand His word without His help; how could we tell Him that He has made a mistake? The only reason we have a category for justice in our minds is because we are image bearers of the only just God. The Lord must teach us true justice and the truth about everything else.

READ JEREMIAH 8:18–9:11. THESE ARE GOD'S WORDS TO ISRAEL WHICH HE SPOKE THROUGH THE PROPHET JEREMIAH. HOW IS THE TENSION BETWEEN JUSTICE AND MERCY PRESENT HERE AS WELL?

NOW READ ISAIAH 53:4–12. IN WHAT WAYS IS THE SAME TENSION PRESENT IN THIS PASSAGE ABOUT JESUS?

WHAT DO WE LEARN ABOUT THE CHARACTER OF GOD FROM TODAY'S PASSAGES? HOW DOES THIS KNOWLEDGE STIR YOUR HEART TO TRUST HIM EVEN MORE DEEPLY TODAY?

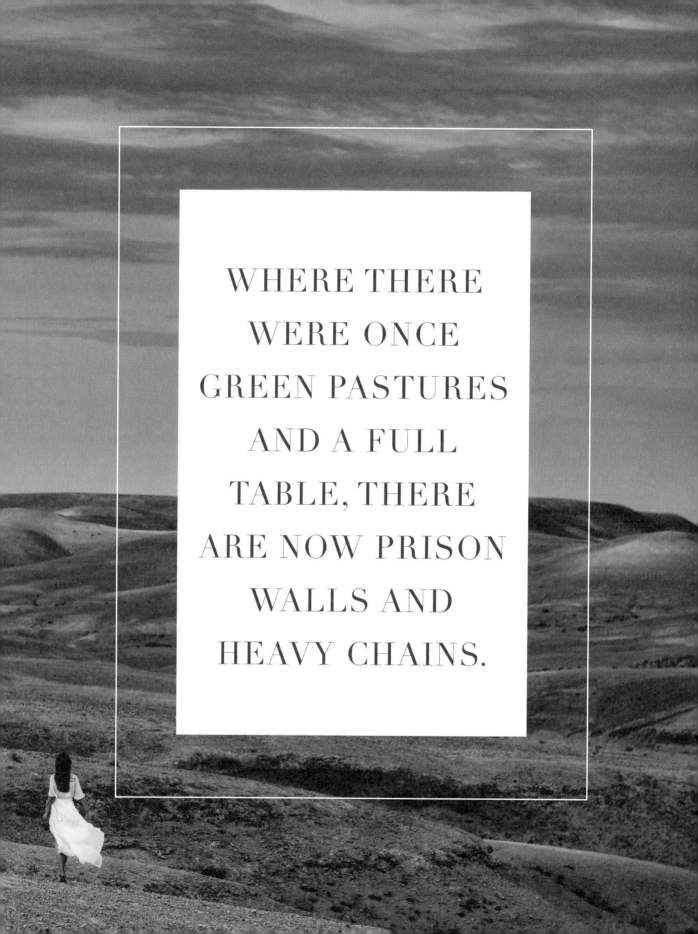

WHERE THERE
WERE ONCE
GREEN PASTURES
AND A FULL
TABLE, THERE
ARE NOW PRISON
WALLS AND
HEAVY CHAINS.

THE GOOD SHEPHERD
Read Lamentations 3:1–9 and Psalm 23

Lady Zion gives her last words at the end of chapter 2. The poet is now speaking again, but now he introduces himself as "the man who has seen affliction." As we have seen, this speaker is evidently both a part of Jerusalem, having personally experienced the events of the siege and exile, as well as someone who speaks to Jerusalem. This third poem is the longest one of the book, and the poet triples the acrostic effect that we have seen in the other chapters. This literary change at the center of the book heightens the emotion of this poem as the author sinks to his deepest despair and rises to his most hopeful point in this middle work.

In the first section of poem three, the author speaks about God as a shepherd who has turned against His own sheep, paralleling Psalm 23 in a dark, contrasting way. Rather than the shepherd who is present to comfort and protect in Psalm 23, we hear about a very different arrangement. The same shepherd, the Lord, is against His sheep in Lamentations. The "rod" of Psalm 23 is a source of comfort and protection from Israel's enemies, but the poet says that this rod is now a means of wrath against Israel. Israel chose to have the shepherd as their enemy; therefore, instead of safety by still waters, the poet speaks of darkness. Israel is the enemy at the table now. The shepherd who provides, shelters, and guides into peace is the One who now afflicts Israel with scarcity, dark dwellings, and a road of bitterness. Where there were once green pastures and a full table, there are now prison walls and heavy chains.

The poet lists more contrasts. In verse 3, he says that God's hand is against him. In Exodus 3:19–20, this same hand was Israel's defense against their Egyptian enemies. The poet of Lamentations also spends three lines talking about walls. These walls are firm and apparently indestructible. Their strength is ironic when we remember the destroyed walls of Jerusalem mentioned in chapter 2. Instead of that wall of defense, the people are barred in by a new kind of barrier, one like a prison wall. Lastly, we hear of Jerusalem's crooked paths in verse 9. In Proverbs 3:6, the Lord declares that those who acknowledge Him in all their ways will have their paths made straight. The city's present condition makes it painfully clear that Jerusalem was not acknowledging the Lord.

What does it mean to acknowledge God in all our ways? In the previous verse in Proverbs, the Lord indicates that trusting in Him is a beginning step in this process. To acknowledge the Lord in all things, we must first trust that He is someone to whom we can go with all things. We need to believe that He is who He says He is. If we believe that God is who He claims to be in Psalm 23, then we should go to Him for everything, because He says that He is the source of fulfillment for all our needs. If we trust that God is good, most wise, and sovereign over everything, then we ought to seek Him in prayer about our thoughts, fears, and plans. Acknowledging the Lord in all our ways also involves confession. If we acknowledge, remember, and act upon the fact that He is involved in every part of our lives, that includes our sin. We have a daily need to confess our sin against Him and accept His grace toward us in Jesus. This is what it means to acknowledge the Lord in all things.

The grief of Lamentations is that God's people did not believe that He was who He said He was or that He would do what He had warned. If the Israelites had acknowledged the Lord in all their ways, they would not have walked so far into darkness and death because of their sin. Had they obeyed and acknowledged Him as their shepherd, He would have led them into straight paths leading to life. But they did not listen to His voice. This passage details what it means to

be without the Good Shepherd. Jerusalem had made themselves His enemies instead. This is exactly the position that we were in before the Lord redeemed our lives, just as He would do one day for the exiled people of Jerusalem. We cannot live rightly without His help.

Christ is the Good Shepherd who guides His people into the only straight path of life. This is not to say that our earthly journey is perfectly pleasant, with no physical or spiritual suffering. In truth, most of the time it is just the opposite. We will actually face hardship because we have aligned ourselves with Christ. Many people do not know God as their shepherd, and instead they know Him, and believers, as enemies. The joy in these trials is that the Good Shepherd is for you, not against you, if you have trusted in what Christ did to reconcile you to the Father. Another joy is that you have the calling to share this gift of life with the world. You get to watch God turn enemy sheep into members of His flock, just like He did for you (Colossians 1:21–22).

The shadow of death mentioned in Psalm 23 and experienced by God's people in Jerusalem during this time is something to be feared only if the Lord is not your shepherd. With Him as your shepherd, it does not mean that you will never walk through such a valley, but it does mean that you have nothing to fear, even in the very depths of one (Psalm 23:4). Jesus's rod and staff are a comfort and defense that you will never lose, because He will never lose His sheep (John 10:28).

To acknowledge the Lord in all things, we must first trust that He is someone to whom we can go with all things.

READ JESUS'S SPEECH IN JOHN 10:1–18.
WHY IS CHRIST A BETTER SHEPHERD
THAN ANY OTHER? WHAT DOES HE DO
FOR AND GIVE TO HIS SHEEP?

READ COLOSSIANS 1:21–23. WHAT HAS
CHRIST DONE FOR YOU?

DO YOU KNOW ANYONE WHO DOES NOT KNOW JESUS AS THEIR GOOD SHEPHERD?
SPEND SOME TIME IN PRAYER FOR THESE PEOPLE, ASKING THE LORD TO GIVE THEM
EYES TO SEE AND A HEART THAT DESIRES TO FOLLOW JESUS.

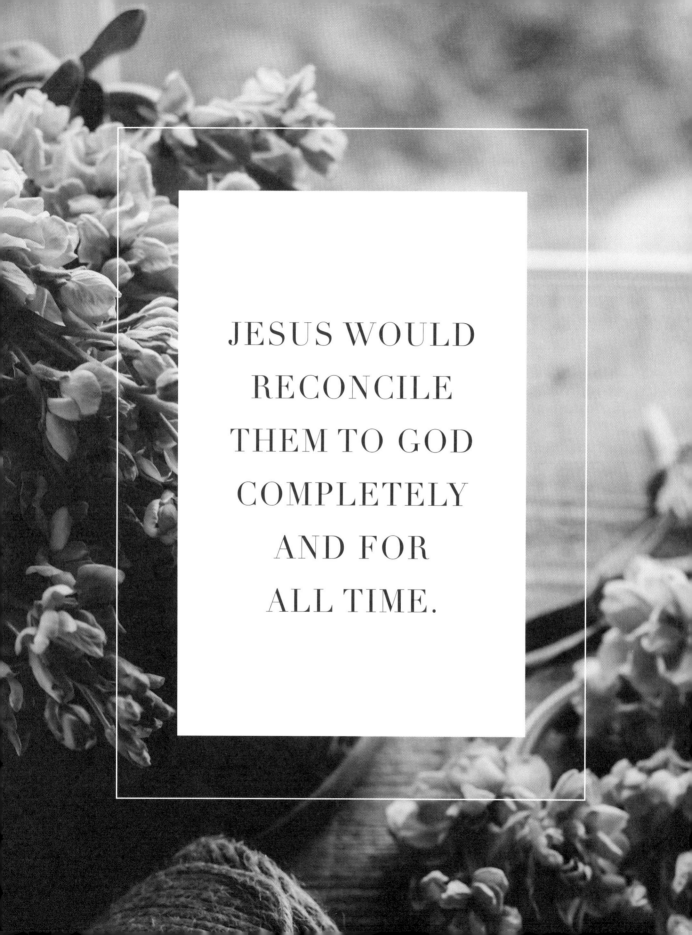

JESUS WOULD
RECONCILE
THEM TO GOD
COMPLETELY
AND FOR
ALL TIME.

A HINT OF HOPE

Read Lamentations 3:10–15 and Psalm 77

The afflicted poet continues to tell of the affliction that has caused his grief. Five out of the six verses from today's reading identify ways that the Lord has wounded the poet. God is described as an animal attacking its prey, just as the prophets warned (Hosea 13:8). He is described as an archer who sends arrows straight into the poet's kidneys. The kidneys are where they once believed the emotions rested, rather than in the heart as we usually say today. God has struck the poet and the people in a way that affected their hearts. This attack was personal because God is a relational God, and Israel had sinned personally against Him.

Verse 14 is the only line in these two stanzas where the poet is the subject. He says that people are mocking and shaming him. It is possible that he is referring to all of Jerusalem being mocked by the surrounding nations, but the word laughingstock is singular. Soon we will see that this poet held onto his hope in God, so it is possible that he personally experienced mocking from his fellow people because of his faith. Either way, he is also dealing with guilt and shame because of sin, and so are the people.

There is a difference between shame and guilt. Adam and Eve felt genuine shame in the garden of Eden, because not only were their physical bodies on display, but their guilt of sin was laid bare too. Jerusalem has been exposed in a similar way. Both parties felt shame because they were guilty of sin. Today, we have no reason to live in shame if we are in Christ. We may be guilty of sin, but in Jesus, we are declared innocent through His cross. Guilt is like a thermometer, and it can be a helpful indicator when there is sin we need to deal with in our lives. Shame is like a thermostat that speaks lies about our identity, telling us how we should feel about ourselves. But if you trust in Jesus, your identity is in Him and His righteousness, not in the lies that shame speaks to you.

After the first fifteen lines of this third poem, it feels as if all that is in the poet's heart and mouth is anger at the Lord. But if we look closer, we hear more of a testimony than an accusation. The poet is listing the many things that he and his city have undergone. All of them are the very prophecies that the Lord gave through the prophets about the coming punishment. The poet is indirectly confessing that the Lord has been faithful to do what He promised. By testifying to what the Lord has done, the poet makes a case for sympathy and fellow grievers.

In Psalm 77, there is similar kind of grief. We do not know what the psalmist is mourning over specifically here. He talks about calling out to the Lord in trouble but refuses to be comforted by Him. When he even thinks about the Lord, he groans, because he knows that God is the one who has afflicted. The same is true for the poet of Lamentations. When he thinks about God, he cannot help but remember what God has done to him and then mourn. The psalmist fires questions in verses 7 through 99, trying to make sense of God's plan. At verse 10 of the psalm, there is a sudden shift to a different kind of remembering.

Neither the psalmist nor the poet look forward with hope yet, because they cannot imagine how their present loss could ever be restored. But the psalmist of Psalm 77 instead begins to look backwards on what the Lord has done before the present circumstances began. First, the psalmist reflects on God's character, and the poet will eventually do the same. Then the psalmist meditates on how God redeemed Israel from their Egyptian enemies and sustained them through trials in the wilderness. He had carried them when they did not understand His plan and even when they felt like He was absent.

Neither the poet nor the psalmist could look back and remember Christ yet, because God's plan to redeem was still playing itself out in the timeline of history. Jesus had not yet come. Israel had heard about Him for centuries and would eagerly wait for Him. But during the exile, all they could see were the depths of their suffering and the impossibility of climbing out of the pit that God had dug for them. But Jesus was coming. He would bear the shame and bitterness of separation from the Lord on behalf of Israel. Jesus would reconcile them to God completely and for all time.

Sometimes in the midst of pain, grief, and even in our sin, it is hard to look forward with hope. It is helpful to instead reflect back on the Lord's past faithful actions and meditate on His character. We can remember those things and sink our grip into them in a way that is often difficult to do when we think about the unknown future. We do not have to use our imagination to look backwards. And as we look back, unlike Jerusalem and the psalmist, we will see Christ. They saw Him when they looked forward in hope, but we live in light of His accomplished work. When you do have those brief moments of strength to look forward, you will see Christ there too. He is sitting on the throne in heaven, ruling and reigning. He will make all things new and will put an end to grief and shame forever.

Neither the psalmist nor the poet could look on their present situation and glean hope from it—they had to look behind or forward to see the light of redemption. As those on this side of the fulfilled covenant, we can look behind and find strength, forward and find hope, but we can also look into the present with peace because Jesus is here with us by His Spirit, if we have trusted in Christ. He has dealt with our guilt and cleansed us so that we have no need to feel ashamed (1 John 1:9). Even as we grieve the realities of this shattered world, we never have to do it without hope.

READ 1 THESSALONIANS 4:13–18. WHAT IS YOUR HOPE IN THE MIDST OF GRIEF?

EVEN THOUGH YOU DO NOT HAVE TO BE ASHAMED ANYMORE, YOU MAY STILL WRESTLE WITH SHAMEFUL FEELINGS. WHAT ARE SOME REASONS FOR THIS?

READ HEBREWS 10:19–25. HOW CAN THESE PROMISES ENCOURAGE YOU WHEN WE EXPERIENCE FEELINGS OF SHAME?

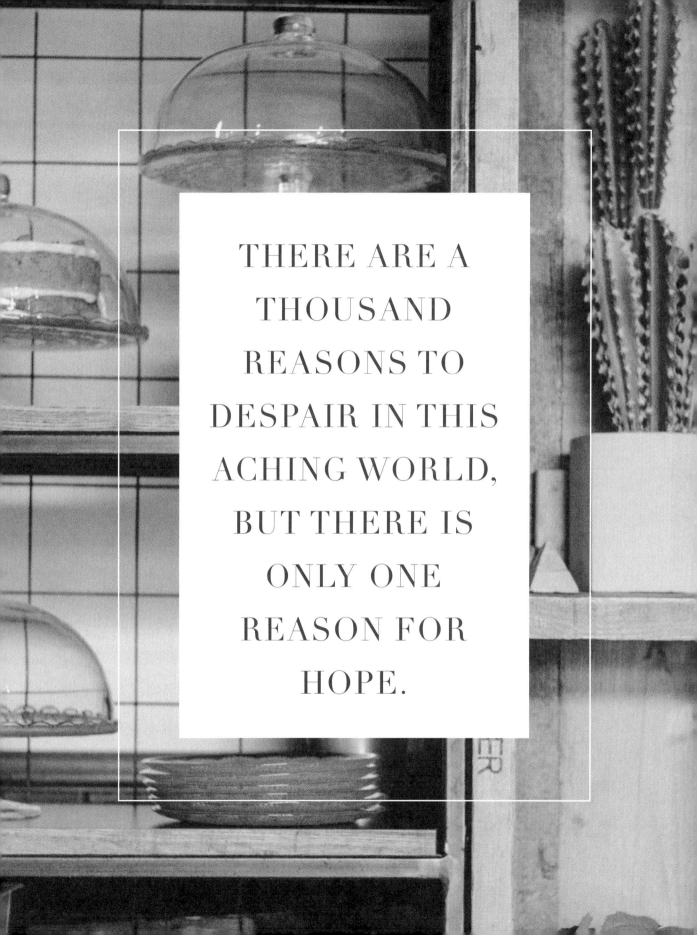

THERE ARE A THOUSAND REASONS TO DESPAIR IN THIS ACHING WORLD, BUT THERE IS ONLY ONE REASON FOR HOPE.

HOPE WHEN WE DON'T FEEL HOPEFUL

Read Lamentations 3:16–18

There is one more detail about the physical torment that Jerusalem has experienced: her people cower in the ashes and dust, with nothing left to consume except rocks. This line may also be a metaphor for the overall experience of punishment that Jerusalem has undergone. She feels as if God has pressed her face down into coarse gravel, which sounds painful and humiliating. But suddenly, the poet transitions to a new aspect of his suffering. He is torn apart inside as well. The Lord has deprived him and the people of peace. True peace is something that only God can give. The poet can no longer remember even what it feels like to be happy. The depth of his present anxiety and sadness seems to make him question if such a feeling even exists.

The tension builds as the poet describes himself sinking deeper into despair. There are no shreds of hope like the ones from Psalm 77. The poet has reached the very depths of depression. He is utterly broken. This is possibly the lowest point in the entire book of Lamentations. Out of his grief, the poet's heart speaks. In his suffering, he allows his emotions to interpret reality, and he sees no hope of a future. Not only this, but he says that in his grief he believed that even his hope of help from the Lord had completely perished. In the following verse, we learn that the poet does not really believe that these despairing thoughts are true; he is just sharing that he has thought them at some point. Not only is there hope, but he sees, knows, and clings to it. He shares his past thoughts with his readers to express the emotional journey that he has experienced.

In the siege and exile of Jerusalem, the poet was stripped of everything he had ever hoped to receive from the Lord's hands: provision, safety, comfort, and peace. His hands are empty, and for a time it felt as though his heart was too. When he says, "My future [splendor] is lost," he appears to refer to the possibility of not only his own existence but that of the world's existence beyond that moment of utter despair. He felt that surely all existence would turn to vapor in mere moments.

It is not clear whether this was intentional or not, but the use of the word Lord, which in Hebrew is *Yahweh,* connotes that there most certainly is hope for tomorrow. The word Yahweh actually comes from the Hebrew verb for existence, "to be." Yahweh means "I am who I am." This is where we get the name of God as "I Am" in Scripture. This name communicates a lot about God and His nature. He is eternal. God has always existed, and He always will exist. Because He is, He has given all other things existence as well. God is the source of all being and all reality. The very mention of His name is a statement that reality will not vanish as the poet fears. Though the earth may fade or be changed, God will always exist.

Even the hopelessness that the poet feels at his lowest point is a merciful gift from the Lord. The poet's greatest need is to know his need for the Lord. Sometimes there is nothing more gracious for the Lord to do than to strip us of the things that we have put our hope and trust in apart from Him. In some cases, this means being brought to the lowest point and then finding that nothing is constant except the Lord. The poet thought that he had lost his hope from the Lord, but truly he was speaking those words out of the sorrow of having lost everything but that. Every possible physical resource, relational support, and temporal blessing had been ripped from his hands. It is in brokenness like this that we treasure what the Lord reveals about Himself as in Psalm 34:18 when the psalmist writes, "The Lord is near the brokenhearted."

There are a thousand reasons to despair in this aching world, but there is only one reason for hope. Jesus is the only thing we can cling to in every season, because He is the only one who will never fade. It is tempting to make hopeless statements out of our pain and to allow feelings of despair to dictate our view of God. This is why we need God's Word. This is why He gave it to you. In it, we can read the truth about the very real hope that we have in Christ and the perfect, unworldly peace that He gives (John 14:27). When we feel like God is not near or that He does not care, truth still remains. Our feelings do not affect the reality of who He is and what He does. The beauty of God's gift of His Word is that we can read it and hear His voice telling us the truth when our fallen emotions often tell us lies. We can read the testimonies of people who have felt the same kind of pain and hopelessness that we may be feeling. We will also hear the truth about the hope we have in the God who gave Jesus and sent His Spirit so that we could have fulfilled hopes for all eternity (John 4:13–14).

The poet still has a great deal to say about hope, but he did not get to that point easily. He wrestled and grieved, and the Lord allows you to do the same. God does not demand that you feel things that you do not genuinely feel. Instead, He walks with you in brokenness and points you to future healing, so that you might have hope in Him.

tetragrammaton (YHWH)

READ EPHESIANS 2:11–22. WHAT IS YOUR HOPE IN THIS LIFE?

WHAT DO TODAY'S PASSAGES REVEAL ABOUT THE CHARACTER OF GOD AND HIS WORD?

IN WHAT WAYS DO YOU NEED TO HOPE IN THE LORD TODAY? SPEND TIME IN PRAYER, ASKING THE LORD TO REMIND YOU OF HIS NEARNESS AND GIVE YOU HOPE.

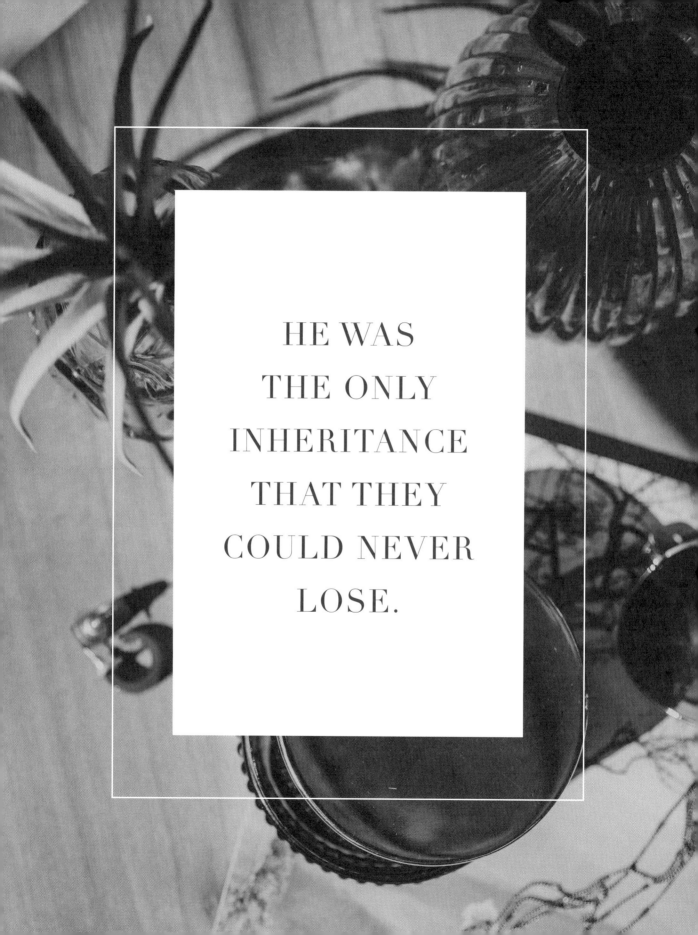

HE WAS
THE ONLY
INHERITANCE
THAT THEY
COULD NEVER
LOSE.

I HAVE A BEAUTIFUL INHFRITANCE

Read Lamentations 3:19–24 and Psalm 16

The horrors of all that Jerusalem and her people have experienced continually flash before the poet's eyes. Even after the events have passed, he cannot get the images out of his head. He does not have to recall the memories to his mind; they are always playing on repeat because remembering the suffering is involuntary. In verse 21, he says that this kind of recollection has only caused him more bitterness and sadness. There is no hope in it.

Suddenly, at this point the tone shifts, and the poet describes another kind of memory. This one is almost forcefully called to his mind. The poet literally has to choose to think about this thought. This other memory is one that gives him hope. After stanza upon stanza of hopelessness and utter despair, could there possibly be something that gives positive expectations here? What is this thought? What does he intentionally remember that gives him hope in the midst of this horrific darkness?

He remembers the steadfast love of the Lord (Exodus 34:6). He recognizes that he and his people have not been totally destroyed, and he attributes this to God's faithfulness. God is faithful in this because the poet and his people deserved to perish for their sin. Considering the terrors that the Lord brought by the weapon of Babylon, it is shocking that there are survivors. Israel was not utterly consumed because the Lord's love for them was steadfast. In order for love to be steadfast, it cannot be based on anything in the object of the love, because those things may change. Our love is not like God's love. Our love is always changing. It is conditional. It varies based on the object of our love which can grow stronger or weaken depending on what it is or does. But God's love for Israel was not based on anything about them; it was based on His steadfast and faithful character (Deuteronomy 7:6–8). He will be faithful in His love to us because that is His character. And this is mercy, because we have never deserved it.

In verse 23, the poet speaks to the Lord for the first time in the book. Up to this point, the poet has spoken about God as the source of all the affliction. He has racked up charges against the Lord as if in a courtroom. But suddenly, the poet has a burst of clarity. It is not that he has forgotten all that the Lord did to him and the city. He cannot forget that reality. Nothing has changed in his situation. But the poet has chosen to see beyond his circumstances and into something more stable. He recognizes that the Lord's mercies are still new every morning. This means that every day the Lord keeps His promises. He is not faithful one day and unfaithful the next. The Lord was faithful to follow through with His promised punishment of the city for their serving of other gods (Psalm 16:4). And now, every day, the poet wakes with breath in his lungs because the Lord is faithful to give Him another day of life.

The poet has a new saying. Rather than the thoughts of despair that spoke lies about the Lord, he now speaks from steady truths instead of his unsteady emotions. He rests in what he knows to be true—the Lord is his portion. This word refers to an inheritance. Before the exile, God's people would probably have said that God's faithfulness meant that they would always have a portion full of food, shelter, clothing, wealth, treasures, and glory. Finally, the poet understands their mistake. They had put all their hope and happiness in earthly things and false gods. Everything that they had once rested in was temporary—it would not last forever. God faithfully removed those things so that His people would see that He was the only inheritance that they could never lose (Ephesians 1:11–14).

In Psalm 16, the psalmist says that He sets the Lord in the front of his mind. Glorifying God is his highest goal. He says that apart from the Lord, He has nothing good. This mindset is similar to the one the poet of Lamentations has been brought to rest in. The poet has learned the hard way that the Lord is his only good and lasting portion and the holder of his lot. His inheritance is the Lord Himself, because the coming of the Savior, Jesus Christ, is his hope for eternal salvation.

The poet challenges his readers' expectations about the faithfulness of God. We hear of no immediate relief or escape from the pain that the poet is going through. Yet, He considers God as faithful and enough for Him. When we reason from our circumstances and present emotions, it is easy to look at what God has placed in our hands and call Him unfaithful because what we find there is not what we want. God not giving you what you want does not equal unfaithfulness. In fact, it means the opposite. God is faithful to keep you from some things that you sinfully desire, because what your flesh naturally wants is sin. Instead, if you have trusted Christ, He has given you His Holy Spirit to live in you through your union with Christ. The Holy Spirit reminds you of God's Word and teaches you to desire righteousness and truth. He teaches you obedience to God's Word, which changes the affections of your heart from wanting the things of earth, to desires to seek and serve Him, and He grants you the ability to begin to do so. In heaven, you will be fully made like Christ and with Him forever. This is your hope and inheritance; He is your portion.

READ EPHESIANS 1:11–14. WHAT IS THE HOPE THAT WE WAIT FOR?

HOW DOES THE REMOVAL OF EARTHLY BLESSINGS IN OUR LIVES PRESS US MORE DEEPLY INTO THE LORD?

HOW IS REMEMBERING A FORM OF OBEDIENCE? HOW CAN YOU PRACTICE REMEMBERING THE TRUTH TODAY?

LAMENTATIONS 3:22

Because of the Lord's faithful love we do not perish, for his mercies never end.

Week Four Reflection

Paraphrase the passage from this week.

_____

_____

_____

_____

_____

_____

_____

_____

_____

_____

_____

_____

_____

What did you observe from this week's text about God and His character?

_____

_____

_____

_____

_____

_____

_____

What does this week's passage reveal about the condition of mankind and about yourself?

How does this passage point to the gospel?

How should you respond to this passage? What is the personal application?

What specific action steps can you take this week to apply this passage?

IT IS BETWEEN
OUR PRAYER
AND GOD'S
ANSWER THAT
HE TEACHES US
ABOUT TRUST.

WAITING IS NEVER WORTHLESS

Read Lamentations 3:25–30 and Isaiah 30

After a startling declaration of hope, the poet describes the Lord and then gives his readers prescriptions for how they should act in response to God's character. Verses 25–27 each begin within the word good in Hebrew: good is the Lord to those who wait, good is it to wait for His salvation, and good is it for a man to bear the yoke in his youth. We have heard that there is hope for Jerusalem, and now the instruction is to wait for it. Wait on the good Lord.

The Lord will be good to the people who wait for him (Isaiah 40:31) and good to those who seek Him (Isaiah 55:6–7). Verse 26 begins a theme of penitence by instructing the readers how they should wait. Waiting for the salvation of the Lord should be done in quietness. Is this a literal or figurative quietness? In some ways, both. The people of Israel are waiting for salvation in the form of deliverance from the suffering their own sin has brought upon them. In this sense, they should literally be silent, willingly bearing the just yoke of their discipline. In another sense, there is also a quietness of heart that should accompany their waiting.

The call to literal quietness does not negate all of the speeches the poet and Lady Jerusalem have given. It is good to cry out to the Lord, as Psalm 62:8 tells us. But now that they have cried out to Him, the poet calls the people of Jerusalem to be silent as they bear the yoke. As we learned earlier, a yoke is used to guide an animal into obedience so that a master can accomplish the work he desires to do through the animal. It is a fitting metaphor for the work that the Lord was doing in Jerusalem during this time. God was refining them. He was clearing out their sin and disciplining them in order to guide them into good paths so that He might carry out His plans in and for them. The Lord disciplines the ones He loves. He did not discipline other nations around Israel in the same way because He did not have a blessed future plan for them as He did for

His covenant people. The yoke God placed on Israel because of their sin is the most merciful thing He could have done for them. He was cleansing them in their youth so they could walk with Him in righteousness for eternity.

The poet tells the people to be literally silent and to put their mouths in the dust. Earlier in the chapter, the poet said that the Lord had pressed their face into the gravel or dust. Dust and ashes are commonly used in Scripture to symbolize repentance (Job 42:6). Initially, the Lord is the one who threw His people into the dust, placing them in a physical position of repentance. Now the poet calls the people to reflect this repentance in their hearts by putting their own mouths into the dust. It is important to recognize the order here. The Lord initiated repentance in the heart of His people. It was not their will power that brought them to this place; it was His mercy and a gracious gift. Repentance—the desire and power to change—is always a gift from God (2 Timothy 2:25). The poet now commands the people to embrace this gift.

In bearing their punishment with quietness and patience, Israel would acknowledge the justice of their punishment. They would learn to trust, honor, and submit to God and His will as they waited for salvation from His hand. They would learn to love and seek the Lord with all their heart, even in the absence of every earthly comfort and even when circumstances did not change. There is purpose in suffering, and there is purpose in waiting for restoration. The works of God always accomplish the purposes of God for the glory of God.

In Isaiah 30:18, we hear something surprising about the Lord during this time: He was waiting too. Isaiah says that God was waiting to be gracious to them. He would rescue and show them His salvation—in His timing. The verse ends with a call to wait on God. Isaiah goes on to reveal all the promises in store for those who wait on the Lord, calling God their Teacher.

Waiting often feels like a middle season in our lives, between the purposes and plans. Waiting itself usually has no purpose in our minds; it is the thing we have to get through to arrive at a purposeful destination. In fact, sometimes we view waiting as the very absence of purpose for a season. This is not how the Lord views waiting.

The Lord accomplishes so much more in our waiting than most of us have ever considered. It is between our prayer and God's answer that He teaches us about trust. It is in trusting Him that He teaches us humility as we see how much higher and better His ways and His timing are than our own (Isaiah 55:8–9). And it is as we learn about God's ways that we fall more deeply in love with Him and fulfill the greatest commandment He ever gave, which is to love the Lord our God fully, with every aspect of our being (Deuteronomy 6:5; Matthew 22:36–37).

Jesus is the hope that the poet ponders but cannot yet name. But we have His history. The poet and his people had only the shadows of Christ through prophecies, and yet even from the literal pit of suffering they learned to trust the Lord in that waiting. They found hope at rock bottom. We have seen that promise of a savior fulfilled, but we are still waiting as well. We wait for the end of suffering, injustice, and brokenness (Isaiah 30:26). We have the gift of faith in Jesus so that we are sustained and sanctified by His Spirit while we wait for the complete fulfillment of our salvation. God uses all kinds of waiting in our lives—from the wait for a spouse, a baby, healing, or even the wait in a traffic jam to refine us into the image of Christ.

READ THE FOLLOWING PASSAGES, AND WRITE DOWN THE PROMISES GIVEN
TO THOSE WHO WAIT ON THE LORD:
PSALM 130, PSALM 25, ISAIAH 33:2, MICAH 7:7

WHY IS IT GOOD TO WAIT ON THE LORD?
WHAT DOES GOD ACCOMPLISH IN
YOUR WAITING?

GOD CAN DO MORE IN YOUR WAITING
THAN IN ANYTHING YOU COULD EVER
ACCOMPLISH IN YOUR ACTION. WHAT
ARE YOU WAITING FOR IN THIS SEASON
OF LIFE? WHAT IS THE LORD TEACHING
YOU DURING THE WAIT?

GOD HAS
BROUGHT
JUDGMENT ON
HIS PEOPLE
DURING THIS
TIME, BUT
HE WILL NOT
REJECT THEM
FOREVER.

HOLY, GOOD, AND LOVING

Read Lamentations 3:–33

There is reasoning behind the hope that the poet has shared. He gave the people of Jerusalem a promise of hope, a method for how to respond to the Lord's gracious character, and now, he gives them the reasoning. Each of the three reasons provides information about what the Lord has done during this time as well as an aspect of His enduring character. The people should have hope and be patient in penitence for several reasons.

First of all, God has brought judgment on His people during this time, but He will not reject them forever. Secondly, God has caused them suffering, but He will again show them merciful compassion. Lastly, God has brought them affliction, but He does not delight in their pain (Hosea 11:8).

All of these reasons for hope and patience in the midst of their suffering reflect aspects of God's eternal nature. In the verses leading up to this passage, the poet reminded His readers that God is faithful (Lamentations 3:22–24) and good (Lamentations 3:25–27). Here he reminds them of God's holiness, goodness, and love. These attributes are visible in the way that God deals with His people's sin. Because God is good and holy, He is rightly angered by injustice. He is also a God who loves His people enough to discipline them so that they might be restored. God's punishment of Israel would give way to merciful compassion. His anger toward them would not persist, but His love would endure forever. God's goodness is not contradictory to His judgment against sin. It is because God is holy, good, and loving that He punished Israel. And God would be holy, good, and loving in His restoration of them.

In verse 33 of our passage, we hear that God does not take joy in the pain that His people are experiencing. God does not enjoy the suffering that each of His individual people are experiencing. But because of His character, God does delight in doing justice. The reality is that God is always holy, good, and loving, even in His anger and wrath against sin. God is all of His attributes, all the time. So there is no part of God that is holy but not good, or loving but not holy, and vice versa. He does not switch between them but holds all His attributes together and embodies all of them simultaneously.

As sinful creatures, this can be difficult to comprehend because we often experience anger that is not loving. But we can look to Christ as one of the greatest examples of God's united holiness, goodness, and love. If God delighted in seeing His people suffer, He never would have sent Christ to redeem them. In love, God the Son bore the painful punishment that our injustice rightly required. God's goodness manifested itself in Christ's suffering, and His love meant Christ's death. The same God whose holiness and goodness were shown in anger toward sinners is the same God whose goodness and love purchased their redemption. He promised from the beginning of the covenant to restore them because of His steadfast love (Deuteronomy 30:1–10). Christ is the evidence that the Lord indeed did not cast Israel off forever. And His Holy Spirit is proof that God is remaking us by His continual work of sanctification in our lives.

The Lord is infinitely compassionate toward us in the struggle against sin and its effects in this broken world. He dealt His wrath upon Jesus so that He might deal tenderly with each of us. We can approach the Lord because He has not cast us off in our sin. We can cling to Him in every season of our lives because He shows abundant, steadfast love toward us. We can cry out to Him when we feel weak or in pain because the Lord does not delight in our suffering. He delights in us (Zephaniah 3:17) because He delights in Christ who bought us back from sin (John 17:23).

We have the Holy Spirit of the living God dwelling in each of us. While our own emotions and actions may not be united and perfect like God in His attributes, we have His Spirit within us. His Spirit is there to remind us of God's love and to teach us how to be like Jesus. As we seek the Lord in His word and through prayer, we will learn more about His great justice and His compassionate mercy. And God's character should always lead us to praise Him, taking delight in worshiping our holy, good, and loving God for who He is and for all that He has done.

God's goodness manifested itself in Christ's suffering,
and His love meant Christ's death.

READ HOSEA 11. WHAT DOES THIS PASSAGE TELL YOU ABOUT GOD'S LOVE FOR HIS PEOPLE?

WHAT DO THESE PASSAGES REVEAL ABOUT GOD'S CHARACTER?

HOW IS IT COMFORTING TO REFLECT ON GOD'S CONSTANT ATTRIBUTES OF HOLINESS, GOODNESS, AND LOVE IN YOUR CURRENT CIRCUMSTANCES?

WE CAN
TRUST GOD'S
PERFECT
CHARACTER.

SOVEREIGN OVER SUFFERING

Read Lamentations 3:34–39

In verses 34–36 of this passage, the poet is clearly speaking on behalf of the people. He lists out things that their enemies have done: The Babylonians have literally crushed them in battle and carried them off as prisoners. They denied them freedom, basic life necessities, and access to the Most High in the temple. There is nothing legal or lawful about what the Babylonians have done to Jerusalem. Their actions were evil.

The poet reminds his readers that all of these actions are things that the Lord does not approve of in His law. The uncomfortable reality is that all the things the poet has just listed are also things that the people of Jerusalem had done before the siege and exile. They had neglected the needy and oppressed, sacrificed their own children to false gods, perverted justice in court, and practiced many other things of which the Lord does not approve. The poet is both accusing his enemies of injustice toward Jerusalem while also exposing Jerusalem as guilty of the same sort of crimes.

The things that have happened to Jerusalem are evils that are not approved by the Lord, and yet they have happened. There is an unspoken plea for God to carry out justice on these things. In verses 37–39, the poet responds to the list of wrongs with the sovereignty and justice of God. First, the poet reminds readers of God's sovereignty. When we say that God is sovereign, it means that He has complete power and control over all things, at all times (Psalm 115:3). In verse 38, the poet carries this truth to its logical end: God controls all things; therefore, both good and bad circumstances come from Him.

There is a challenging mystery to God's sovereignty. God is not evil, and He does no evil. God did not create sin, and He never sins. But He has control over all things, including sin. So when the Israelites are experiencing injustice at the hands of their enemies, the Lord is present in this reality (Amos 3:6). God has allowed wicked Babylon to unleash evil onto Jerusalem. The Lord used their sin to carry out His judgment, but He did not cause them to sin. God Himself is not evil or unjust when He allows these injustices to take place. In fact, He is just for punishing Israel's own wickedness. We will never fully understand God's sovereign rule, but we can trust His perfect character.

The book of Job discusses the mystery of God's sovereignty over suffering. Job was a righteous man who feared the Lord, but God allowed Satan to take family, treasures, and health from Job. Even after he lost almost everything that mattered to him, Job blessed the Lord. He said, "Should we accept only good from God and not adversity?" (Job 2:10). Job understood that he was a created being and that God was the Creator who had the right to do with Job as He saw fit. This righteous man's suffering also reveals that we cannot earn security or salvation and that a right relationship with the Lord does not mean freedom from earthly trouble. Job was innocent of sin in this instance, and yet he rested in the Lord's goodness in the midst of his pain. But here we see Jerusalem, filthy with sin, and yet they complained about their circumstances.

Jerusalem's own sin led to the painful realities they faced. The poet highlights this fact in verse 39. He asks why living people, created beings, are complaining to the Creator, especially when they are bearing the rightful punishment for their actions. Jerusalem naturally wants to be rescued from the injustice that Babylon continues to do against them. Throughout Lamentations we can hear them struggling with God's timeline. They understand His punishment, and they recognize that they deserved it. But now that they have been punished, they long to see their enemy defeated. They do not understand God's timeline. They want Him to judge Babylon immediately. But the Lord was patient with Israel for centuries during their own injustices. He waited for generations to finally execute judgment on them because He showed forbearance toward them in love. God does not love Babylon like He loves Jerusalem, but He is patient in dealing with them as well.

God saw both the injustice that Israel committed and the sin that He allowed Babylon to commit against Israel. In His righteousness, God would deal with both (Psalm 92:5–9). And in His timing, God eventually rescued Israel from the hand of the Babylonians, and He renewed His promises to redeem them from all their earthly enemies, including the enemy of their own sin.

Jesus came many years later to fulfill these promises. By dying on the cross at the hands of sinful people, Christ bore the punishment for all our injustice. We see the same justice conflict when we look to the cross. Jesus bore our sins. His sacrificial death brought justice. But in being the innocent, perfect, matchless Son of God, His death was the greatest injustice. The truth is, Jerusalem deserved far worse than they got. They deserved to be totally annihilated because of their sin against a holy God (Romans 6:23). And so do we (Romans 3:23).

Even in Jesus's death on the cross, God in His sovereignty used our sin to carry out His good purposes. Jesus died at the hands of sinful men in order to purchase your redemption because that was God's sovereign plan. God uses your sin for His glory. This does not make your sin good in any way; it merely demonstrates the supreme goodness of God. He did this to secure your freedom from sin. Even though you still fight sin on earth, you can be confident that God will use your mistakes and give you victory for His glory.

READ PSALM 92:5-15. WHY DO YOU NOT NEED TO FEAR WHEN EVIL SEEMS TO PROSPER IN THE WORLD?

WHAT DOES THIS PASSAGE REVEAL ABOUT THE CHARACTER OF GOD?

HOW CAN GOD'S SOVEREIGNTY COMFORT YOU TODAY?

JESUS'S
PERFECTLY
RIGHTEOUS
RECORD IS
THE ONE
THAT STANDS
FOREVER IN
OUR PLACE.

FOR HIS GLORY
Read Lamentations 3:40–51 and Daniel 9:1–19

Just as he called his readers to a posture of repentance in verses 28–30, the poet now summons the people to active repentance which involves confession and change. He includes himself in the command this time by using the first-person pronoun, us. He says that they all need to examine themselves and go back to seeking God. They should lift their hands and their hearts in prayer to God. There needs to be heart change, not only lip-service. This is what true repentance looks like for Israel and for us. Surprisingly, the prayer that follows is not a prayer of repentance but one of continued grief and accusations against the Lord. It sounds like the start of repentance when they confess their sin and rebellion in the first line, but it quickly gives way to frustration instead of a plea for forgiveness.

The author is right that God has not yet forgiven them, because if he had done so already, the punishment would have ended. But the people have not yet asked for forgiveness. They have grieved their punishment, listed their sorrows, and even have come so far as to confess that they sinned against the Lord. But at this point in the book, there has been no plea for restoration. Right now they can only weep, hoping to receive the renewal of the Lord's tender compassion, because they were not experiencing it in the same way during exile as they had for so many years before.

The prayer is steeped in continued confusion at the Lord's actions. God appears to have wrapped Himself in His own anger like a garment. The cloud that had once been a symbol of God's presence and His protection of Israel when He led them through the wilderness is now the symbol of God's wrath against them. The Lord is no longer attentive to their prayers, and the other nations have noticed. The city of the Most High God has been disgraced, and its people are devastated and humiliated. How their hearts must have ached feeling cut off from their God.

The poet himself literally cannot stop crying because of this. His tears are a plea for the Lord to act on their behalf. This is a fulfillment of prophecy. God said through Jeremiah that His people would eventually return to Him, weeping over sin as they came (Jeremiah 50:4–5). Just as the Lord foretold their punishment, He had also given prophecies about their deliverance. The people of Israel needed reconciliation with God, because once restored, they could pray, and the Lord would again attend to their voices. Right now, all they seem able to do is weep.

Daniel's prayer in Daniel 9 is an example of genuine self-examination and repentance, both for Israel and for us. Daniel was one of the Israelites taken to Babylon. He was a prophet who fiercely served the Lord, and yet we hear him confessing the guilt of his sin right along with the sin of his people. He does not make excuses as he declares the Lord righteous in all of His judgments against Jerusalem. At the end of his prayer of confession, Daniel pleads with the Lord to show mercy on His wounded people for the sake of His great name. The nations that the poet of Lamentations mentioned are mocking the Lord because they see His people destroyed. Daniel pleads that the Lord would act, not because they are righteous or deserving but because they are the city called by God's name.

The Lord is a compassionate God who delights in rescuing the needy and oppressed, but He is also a holy God who is jealous for the glory of His name. He gave His name to Israel so that they would be called His people. When the Lord eventually arises to rescue Jerusalem from Babylon, it will be on account of His name (Isaiah 48:9–11). God would also give them new hearts so that they could have genuine repentance. For those who have trusted Christ, God has given a new heart too. The truth is that Israel would never repent perfectly enough on their own to deserve the Lord's favor, as Lamentations exemplifies. This is why it is mercy that the Lord dealt with Israel and us, not on account of our sin but for the sake of His glory.

God's glory is our shield. In love He called a people by His name long ago when He chose Israel. Even while the poet pleaded, the Lord was already looking down and seeing their desolation. He had a plan to vindicate them and His name, for His own glory. This is the wayward people group He chose to redeem and make new. Jesus would come one day to live a sinless life so that God's people might be known, not only by His name but also by His righteousness instead of their impurity. Those who trust in Jesus are now representatives of God's glory to the world. The difference is that we cannot mess it up, like Israel. This is not because we will never sin—we will sin until we are made new in heaven. Rather, Jesus's perfectly righteous record is the one that stands forever in our place, and all our sin has been nailed to the cross.

If you believe in Jesus, the Lord's tender compassion for you will never end, because you are united to Christ. Christ's righteousness is yours, so you will never have to face God's wrath or the rejection of your prayers because of your sin. He has given you a new heart and the gift of repentance so that you can come before the Lord at all times to confess your sins and receive His grace to teach you how to walk away from them. God has compassion on you in your weakness to fight sin and the suffering you experience in a sinful world. You can ask Him for help and comfort, and He will always hear you. In truth, He has already answered every need you could ever bring before Him, through Jesus. Because of Jesus, you know God and are known by Him even now. You have been raised from death to eternal life. In heaven, you will fully experience that life with no more sin in the way. And in all this, God is greatly glorified.

READ 2 PETER 3:10–13. HOW SHOULD YOU STRIVE TO LIVE IN LIGHT OF WHAT CHRIST HAS DONE?

WHAT DOES THIS PASSAGE REVEAL ABOUT GOD'S CHARACTER?

WRITE A PRAYER, PRAISING GOD FOR THESE ASPECTS OF HIS CHARACTER.

GOD'S
FAITHFULNESS
IS GREATER
THAN OUR
SUFFERING.

A PATTERN OF DELIVERANCE

Read Lamentations 3:52–58

Remember that the author of Lamentations uses three different perspectives in his writing. The first is his own personal voice and experience, the second is the female personification of Jerusalem, and the third is when he speaks corporately on behalf of all the people in the city. In verses 52–58, the poet gives his personal testimony. This seems to be a story about an experience the poet has had in the past when he was in some sort of danger that should certainly have ended in death, but the Lord rescued him.

These verses may suggest that Lamentations was indeed written by Jeremiah, since there is an account in Jeremiah 38 where the prophet is thrown into a literal pit. Jeremiah was also hunted for no reason because he was persecuted for trying to tell the people of Jerusalem the truth. And the Lord rescued Jeremiah from that pit, just as the poet speaks about being rescued from his pit in verse 58. There are many similarities.

We still cannot say for sure if the poet is Jeremiah, but whoever is telling this story uses a pattern common in the book of Psalms to describe deliverance. The poet calls out to God, the Lord hears, the Lord comes near, and the Lord delivers and redeems. In the memory, the Lord took up his cause and redeemed him. While his present experience feels like another inescapable pit, the poet looks back, allowing the past to interpret the present. This remembering should be habitual for every believer. We cannot interpret God and His character based on our present pain. Instead, we need to interpret all our circumstances based on knowledge of God from His Word and from the evidence of His past faithfulness. Circumstances change, but God does not.

If we are confident in our knowledge of the Lord's character, we will call out to Him in times of need, just like the poet in verse 55. Even from the deepest part of a pit, he called on the name of the Lord. The metaphor of a pit is used often in Scripture to describe trouble or total despair (Psalm 88; Job 33:28). God has cast the poet into the pit of exile in Babylon even as he writes this, but in the memory and in the rest of the chapter, God is no longer described as the enemy. The poet now recognizes God as his only true deliverer. He understands that God was faithful long before this suffering ever took place, and He would be the same in the midst of it. God's words are always steadfast, even when our circumstances shift (Isaiah 40:8).

The reality is that God's faithfulness is greater than our suffering, even when He leaves us in it. But He will not leave us in it forever. The book of Psalms is filled with the cries of God's people trusting in the Lord to fulfill His promises. The fact is that God's promises, when they are given, always have a future fulfillment. For example, God has promised to deliver us, and we witness this already in the deliverance we have experienced from our slavery to sin, but we will see His deliverance ultimately fulfilled in heaven when we are totally free. There will be no more need for promises in heaven because we will behold their fulfillment with our eyes forever.

The command, "Do not fear," is used more than any other command in Scripture. Sometimes it is followed by immediate deliverance like in the poet's testimony in verses 52–57. But more often, the command to not be afraid is given at times when, humanly speaking, there are more than a few reasons to genuinely fear danger. When God tells us not to fear, it often has little to do with our circumstances and much more to do with His sufficiency to protect us from anything that might be a cause for fear. This very command is given in verse 57, and it is the only direct quote we have from the Lord in the whole book of Lamentations.

So maybe you are weary of hanging on to promises for rescue from what feels like a pit in your life. Maybe you just want the brokenness to be healed now. You want all causes for fear to be gone in your life, not a command to live as if they already are. Maybe it is hard to remember times when you have seen God deliver you like He did for the poet. You may resonate with Psalm 88, the only psalm without a single stanza of hope. Its writer feels completely abandoned and left for dead; there is no pattern of deliverance. He describes himself in a pit as well, with the Lord against him, rather than hearing, drawing near, and delivering. While there may be seasons this feels true, the truth is that if you are in Jesus, you have never and will never experience utter despair.

You may struggle with despairing feelings and even depression, which are real and challenging battles, but the only person who has ever experienced the genuine pit of utter despair is Jesus. When He bore the fullness of your sins on the cross, the Father had to turn His face away from His Son. But because sin and death cannot hold Christ, He rose again. When Jesus emerged from the pit of the grave, your sin was no longer on Him. The Father now looks on Jesus and is satisfied. So when the Father sees those who are in Christ, He sees the perfection of His Son. Even though you live in a world that often feels like a pit because of sin, you must remember this: God redeemed Jesus from the pit, and if you are in Christ, you will one day be fully redeemed from it too. It may be fearsome, but you have no need to fear.

The truth is that God preserves those who trust in Him (Jeremiah 39:18). God was teaching Israel how to be the people who trusted in Him, even as He disciplined them in Babylon. You may wrestle daily to trust the Lord completely, but Jesus has trusted Him perfectly for you. And while you may not see the redemption part of the deliverance pattern with your eyes yet, you can rest in the Lord who has already come near to you, through His son and in His Spirit. And as you imitate Jesus, you will learn to trust Him in every stage of the pattern.

READ PSALM 34. HOW IS THE PATTERN OF THIS PSALM SIMILAR TO THE PATTERN OF CALLED, HEARD, CAME NEAR, AND REDEEMED FROM TODAY'S PASSAGE?

WHAT ARE SOME STRUGGLES IN YOUR LIFE THAT YOU LONG TO SEE THE LORD REDEEM OR RESCUE YOU FROM?

HOW CAN THE PROMISE OF THE LORD'S NEARNESS AND THE HOPE OF WHAT CHRIST HAS DONE COMFORT YOU IN EACH OF THOSE STRUGGLES?

LAMENTATIONS 3:23

They are new every morning; great is your faithfulness!

Week Five Reflection

Paraphrase the passage from this week.

_____
_____
_____
_____
_____
_____
_____
_____
_____
_____
_____
_____
_____
_____
_____

What did you observe from this week's text about God and His character?

_____
_____
_____
_____
_____
_____
_____
_____

What does this week's passage reveal about the condition of mankind and about yourself?

_____

_____

_____

_____

How does this passage point to the gospel?

_____

_____

_____

_____

_____

How should you respond to this passage? What is the personal application?

_____

_____

_____

_____

What specific action steps can you take this week to apply this passage?

_____

_____

_____

_____

_____

VENGEANCE
BELONGS
TO THE LORD.

THE PATIENCE OF THE LORD
Read Lamentations 3:59–66

Today we will look more intently at the poetic patterns in these verses. Hebrew poetry is marked by various kinds of parallelism. Parallelism means that the individual lines have significant relationships with one another. In the last section of poem three, the poet states truths about the Lord and builds his readers' confidence in coming salvation. Instead of personal testimony, the poet now shares a corporate prayer, speaking on behalf of the people of Jerusalem.

In verse 59, there is an instance of consequential parallelism. This means that the second line is a consequence of the first line. Try inserting the word "therefore" between the lines: "Lord, you saw the wrong done to me; [therefore] judge my case." The poet knows that God sees all things; therefore, he considers the Lord a fitting judge. He seems confident that God will act in favor of His people because of the wickedness of the Babylonians.

The poet says that the Lord has seen and heard everything that the enemies of Jerusalem have done. In fact, the Lord knows even more than the poet and the people do, because He has heard the plotting of the enemies in secret. This is a reference to the fact that God is omniscient, which means that He is all-knowing. This reminder of God's omniscience is reminiscent of the time when the Israelites were in bondage in Egypt. They cried out for rescue, and in Exodus 2:25, God heard their cries, and He knew. He saw the injustice and their need, and He delivered them.

Fast-forward centuries later, and the Israelites have found themselves in bondage once again. They are crying out to the Lord just as they were back in Egypt. The mocking and attacking from their new enemy is going on continually, without reprieve. In verse 63, there appears to be an example of temporal parallelism. The poet speaks of the enemy sitting and rising, a metaphor for something happening constantly. What is happening all the time? The people are being "mocked by their songs." There is so much shame and humiliation behind the words of these few verses.

The poet acknowledges the Lord's omniscience, yet the sense of discouragement is heavy, especially in verses 62–63. In these two verses, God is no longer the subject as before. Rather than returning to the comforting theme of the Lord's omniscience, the poet seems to briefly get lost in descriptions of his relentless enemies.

In the final stanza, the poet's corporate prayer returns to a focus on what the Lord will do rather than on what Israel's enemies have done. Verse 64 reveals that Israel's enemies will receive payback in the exact amount that they deserve; however, this justice will not be immediately visible. The Lord's curse is indeed on His enemies, as the poet pleads, and one day He will bring about that full, deserved judgment. But in the same way that the Lord was slow to judge Israel, so He does not immediately lay final judgment on their enemies.

The Lord's forbearance toward sinners is because of His mercy. In the New Testament, Peter explains the Lord's slowness to bring about the final judgment. It seems like a slow process from our perspective, but Peter says that this is really the Lord's patience toward us. He wants to draw people into salvation in Christ before judgment comes on those who have not put their trust in Him (2 Peter 3:9). The Lord did not bring full punishment on Israel because He was planning to lay it on Jesus. And through Jesus, He will bring final judgment on all His enemies. He was not waiting to save Babylon. He was waiting to send Jesus. And even today, the Lord has not brought final judgment on the earth because He is patient with sinners and desires to draw many to Himself through what Christ has done.

Most of us have probably never experienced the degree of suffering or injustice that the poet grieves over here, so some of his sentiments may seem harsh to us. But most of us have felt pain or oppression at some point in our lives, and if not, we have certainly seen our fellow humans deal with those things in terrible ways. It is natural to desire justice for those people in the form of their deliverance and the punishment of the ones who have afflicted them. An important thing to notice though is that the poet recognizes that the Lord is the one who will punish the enemies, not he or his people. Vengeance belongs to the Lord (Deuteronomy 32:35). There are times when the Lord will call His people to carry out justice on earth for the sake of the oppressed, but ultimate vengeance belongs to Him. We must wait for the day when He will bring it about completely.

In the meantime, you can pray to that end just like the poet, resting confidently in the fact that our omniscient God sees and knows about modern injustice too; He will deal with it perfectly. But when the omniscient God looked at the broken world, He also saw that its real sickness was sin. He did not propose a temporary, patched-up solution that would only deal with earthly injustice while ignoring the root of the problem. Instead, God sent Jesus to deal with your greatest enemy—sin—and to teach you how to live justly in your daily life until His ultimate day of justice.

The Lord did not bring full punishment on Israel because He was planning to lay it on Jesus.

READ MICAH 6:8. WHAT IS YOUR CALLING AS A FOLLOWER OF GOD?

READ 2 PETER 3. WHAT DOES PETER ENCOURAGE US TO DO AS WE WAIT FOR THE LORD TO JUDGE THE EARTH AND ITS INJUSTICE?

HOW HAS THE LORD DELIVERED YOU FROM SIN AND SLAVERY TO INJUSTICE? HOW HAVE YOU SEEN HIS PATIENT MERCY TOWARD YOU?

HOW CAN YOU PRAY FOR THE OPPRESSED TODAY, ASKING THE LORD TO DELIVER THEM FROM BOTH PHYSICAL HARM AND THEIR SICKNESS OF SIN?

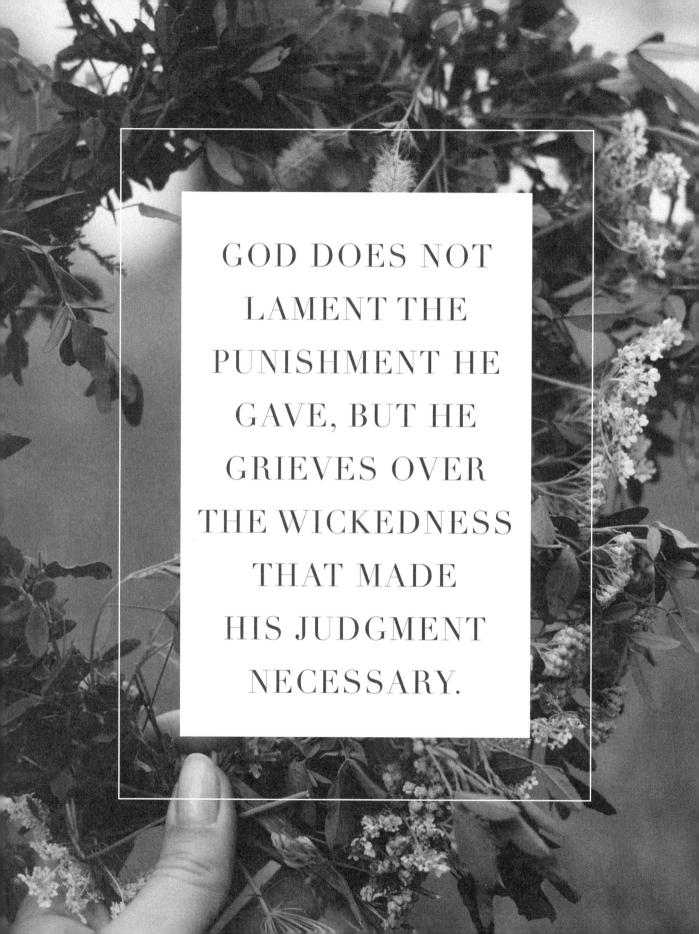

GOD DOES NOT LAMENT THE PUNISHMENT HE GAVE, BUT HE GRIEVES OVER THE WICKEDNESS THAT MADE HIS JUDGMENT NECESSARY.

WHERE WORTH COMES FROM

Read Lamentations 4:1–10 and Jeremiah 2

Just as chapter 1 opened the book, this chapter begins with the corruption that has gone on in the city of Jerusalem. While this fourth poem follows the acrostic pattern of the previous three chapters, it is much shorter than any of them. There is also less emotion in these short stanzas—as if the poet is too exhausted to continue. Glory has departed from Jerusalem, literally, in the loss of the Lord's gracious presence, and the results are almost too horrific to read.

The first two stanzas are filled with imagery of gold, which was the most valuable item the city possessed. Gold was also what lined the garments of the priests in the temple, so it symbolizes holiness in addition to wealth. But instead of adorning the priestly vestments, this gold is scattered in the streets. In verse 2, the poet reveals that the objects of gold are really symbolic of something more valuable—human lives. The people of Jerusalem who have been victims of the sword and of famine have been trampled in the roads. These men and women were once valued more than gold by God Himself, but they have become like discarded pottery.

This theme of priceless things being devalued runs all throughout the first ten verses of the chapter. Mothers are compared to ostriches, an animal who does not care for its young. Babies' who once were well fed, now have mouths so dry and weak that they cannot even call out for their needs. The rich have become poor, and those who once wore purple clothing, the color of wealth, now cling to ashes instead.

The poet interjects amid the descriptions to say that their punishment has been worse than that of Sodom. When God judged the city of Sodom, He destroyed it in an instant. But Jerusalem is dying slowly. Sodom also had no one to grieve for her because she was a city full of horrific wickedness. The story of its downfall is found in Genesis 19 and would have been a common referent for readers of Lamentations. Jerusalem once had great value as a city of God, but now they are slowly fading away. This loss was cause for immense grief. It is also important to notice that what gave Jerusalem worth was not the degree of wealth she possessed; being the recipient of God's covenant love and care gave the city value.

Jerusalem had been filled with beautiful people but not just physically appealing. Her people were once pure, which is what the poet means when he says that they were whiter than milk. Along with physical strength, their hearts were strong with love for the Lord. But now in place of purity there is darkness, blacker than soot. Instead of the former reputation for purity and beauty, the people of Israel are unrecognizable. Not only has their physical appearance degraded, but when they forsook the Lord, they also forfeited the inward value that He gave them. In response to this, the poet repeats the refrain that it would have been better to die swiftly at the hand of a sword like Sodom than to be starved to death in this way.

The poet ends his descriptions here with a phrase that is literally translated, "daughter of my people." It is easy to skim over this line and think that the poet is simply voicing his own grief. But we have to remember that God is ultimately the author of all of Scripture. These are His people. God does not lament the punishment He gave, but He grieves over the wickedness that made His judgment necessary. Jeremiah 2 recounts some of the former glory of Jerusalem and the gifts they lost by straying from the Lord. The whole chapter sounds like the letter of a sorrowful lover who is mourning the loss of his former bride.

The third verse of that letter reads, "Israel was holy to the Lord." The past tense cannot be ignored. The Lord says that His people sought after worthless things such as idols made out of human hands and nations who had no value because they did not know the Lord. In seeking after these things instead of God, the people themselves became worthless, just like the things they pursued (Jeremiah 2:5). God calls his people out for this directly in verse 11, saying that they have traded the glory they possessed through His presence and His many gifts for things that literally bring them nothing. The Lord tried to lead them in the way to life, but instead they chose to walk in the way that leads to death (Jeremiah 2:23). In Jeremiah 2:31, God asks His people a rhetorical question: "Have I been a wilderness to Israel or a land of dense darkness?" The obvious answer is no. God

has lavished them with life and good gifts, but Israel acted as if the glory and blessing of the Lord were trials to endure. They kicked and screamed like toddlers who moan over the food their parents give them for sustenance.

The clear reality of these passages is that all value is found in the Lord. Worth comes from seeking things that have value. God is the only one of value—the only one worth seeking. We were once hopeless and without God, too, like Sodom or Jerusalem (Ephesians 2:12). But Christ purchased our worth at the cross. When you trust in Him, He gives you value and meaning to your life. But if we reject Him and the gifts that He holds out, we ourselves become worthless. Every other pursuit brings death. During the exile, Jerusalem's glory was turned to shame. They lost what only God could restore to them. Jesus paid for it with His life so that His supreme value might be our own and so that the Father could call us His people forever. The Lord is remaking His people into a spotless bride, whose beauty and value will be eternally restored (Ephesians 5:26–27).

If you are seeking value in things other than God's Word and your salvation in Jesus, then let these passages remind you of the truth. Any other pursuit is not only worthless, but it will leave you empty too. If you are in Christ, you are more precious than gold or any other costly substance to your heavenly Father. Say that to yourself when you feel tempted to seek out your worth on social media, through the approval of others, from the grades you get or the money you have, by landing that new job or better body, or whatever it is that you hold up as a false standard to measure your value. His work is the only thing you really have to boast about, because what He has done is what gives you supreme worth. What the world thinks of you means nothing when you have the approval of the one true God through His perfect Son's sacrifice for your life.

READ EPHESIANS 2:1-10. WHERE DOES YOUR WORTH COME FROM?

HOW DO THE PRIORITIES IN YOUR LIFE NEED TO CHANGE TO REFLECT THE WORTH YOU HAVE IN CHRIST?

LIST SOME OF THE THINGS PEOPLE THINK GIVE THEM VALUE IN THIS WORLD. HOW ARE THESE THINGS REALLY WORTHLESS PURSUITS COMPARED WITH THE RICHES THAT COME FROM SEEKING GOD?

IF WE KNOW
JESUS, GOD
REGARDS CHRIST
AND HIS WORK
INSTEAD OF
OUR OWN.

PROPHET, PRIEST, AND KING JESUS

Read Lamentations 4:11–16

When the poet says that God has emptied His anger in full, this does not mean that God has poured out the fullness of His wrath against sin. If He had, Jerusalem would have been utterly wiped out. The entirety of God's wrath has only ever been laid on Christ. He did, however, fully release the anger He had toward Jerusalem for their wickedness and their rejection of His words of warning. The beauty of this line is that it reveals that there is an end to God's anger. It does not last forever (Malachi 3:17). This truth is in stark contrast to God's tender mercy, which has no end point. It can never be exhausted or fully spent.

So even as the poet begins verse 11 with the reminder of God's anger, he shares with us that the end is in sight. Nonetheless, a physical fire from the hand of Babylon has consumed the city to its foundations, which means that the damage is not just superficial. And yet the spiritual fire of God's anger is far more injurious. God's fury may be finished, but could the people possibly rebuild with their hands and hearts now singed by the flames?

The poet goes on to explain that Jerusalem's leaders were the cause for God's heated anger. Kings, prophets, and priests were responsible for leading and guiding God's people in obedience and love toward Yahweh. The kings did not believe God's warnings about the coming punishment. Jerusalem was the city where God's people dwelled and where Yahweh Himself resided. Even the nations knew of the prosperous protection that God gave to these people. No one saw this coming, the poet mourns. But that is the point. The leaders did know it was coming. It is clear by now that God had warned Israel in many ways about the consequences of continuing their wicked lifestyle. The prophet Jeremiah spoke those very prophecies to Jerusalem for forty years. But the kings literally could not believe it was possible that God would harm His own holy city. Oh, how they had forgotten their covenant bonds.

Next, the poet says that the sins of the prophets and priests were also a reason for God's flaming judgment. The prophets who spoke false words of peace should have shouted warnings and encouraged obedience. The priests who ought to have dealt with the stains of unclean citizens became defiled themselves with the blood of the righteous people they killed. The priests may have literally murdered innocent people, but this might also be a metaphor for how they worshiped and served false gods in the temple.

In verses 14 and 15, the poet reveals the ironic consequences of the leaders' failures. The men who once saw visions from the Lord and acted as guides for the people now stagger blindly through the streets, unable to discern their own path. The priests are covered with blood and are therefore unclean. They are so unclean that even unclean people from other nations will not approach them. The sad truth is that the priests were the very ones who should have cleansed others of their sin and uncleanness. They should have sent people away who were unclean in order to deal with their impurity and guide them into restoration. But now, the priests themselves are being sent away by unclean people, and the Lord has rejected them from His presence. He will not acknowledge them anymore or consider their sacrifices because they did not acknowledge Him.

The leaders who once received honor from the people and favor from the Lord because of their high positions now bear the weight of the great responsibility they had. The higher the status, the greater the fall. If the Lord will not regard the king, then how can the city be sure of their safety from other nations? If the Lord will not acknowledge the prophets, how will the people hear from the Lord? If God will not recognize the priests, how can the people be cleansed? In time, God would restore these positions and again regard His people and their leaders. But

the fear of another failure must have hung heavy in the hearts of Jerusalem's inhabitants as they waited for Messiah's coming.

When Messiah finally came, He fulfilled the covenant perfectly on behalf of Israel, which is why He is known as the true Israel. He also is a better prophet, priest, and king on our behalf than any who came before Him. Jesus always spoke the word of the Lord rightly (John 12:49), as a prophet is called to do. He was the spotless Lamb for the priestly sacrifice that we needed because of our sin (1 Peter 1:19), and now He is our Great High Priest forever (Hebrews 7:21). And Jesus is seated now in heaven on the throne, reigning as King of all kings (Revelation 17:14).

The earthly prophets, priests, and kings were but shadows of the true realities that Jesus has always embodied. If we know Jesus, God regards Christ and His work instead of our own. His perfection covers tenfold over the failures of former and present leaders. What a mercy this is, because in our constant struggle to fight indwelling sin, we face the reality of many more fallen leaders in both the secular sphere and even in the church. Modern political figures and the pastors of local churches are not faultless or innocent. Some are even guilty of gravely violating their sensitive roles.

Every earthly leader can and will fail in some way. But praise the Lord that we are not to put our trust in any human man or institution. As a follower of Jesus, we are called to place our hope for salvation in Christ alone, not in a political leader and not in our pastors. Leaders in this world are given by God, but they are sinful humans, too. But Jesus is our perfect leader. He will neither oppress nor abuse. He will never fail to fulfill His responsibility. As we look to Him, we will find Him forever faithful, even amidst the unfaithfulness of earthly leaders.

HOW ARE WE TEMPTED TO PLACE OUR HOPE OR TRUST IN MODERN DAY LEADERS INSTEAD OF IN THE LORD?

READ THE FOLLOWING PASSAGES ABOUT JESUS, AND WRITE DOWN WHAT THEY TELL YOU ABOUT HIS ROLE:

ACTS 3:22–26

HEBREWS 4:14–16

REVELATION 17:14

HOW IS THE LORD A BETTER HOPE THAN ANY EARTHLY LEADERS?

PROPHET, PRIEST, AND KING JESUS

Throughout Lamentations and all of Scripture, we hear of three
central kinds of leaders: prophets, priests, and kings. In various ways,
the men who filled these roles throughout the Old Testament failed
to do so perfectly and were really just shadows of a truer and better
prophet, priest, and king who would one day come to perfectly fulfill
each of the needs that these offices were designed to meet.

	PROPHET	PRIEST	KING
JERUSALEM	*Their prophets told lies and did not speak God's word to the people.* (Jeremiah 5:31)	*Their priests offered sacrifices to false gods and were too sinful to even make atonement for the sins of the people.* (Lamentations 4:13–14)	*The kings in the land were not concerned with the safety of their people and allowed them to spiral into destruction instead of leading them to listen to the Lord.* (Lamentations 4:12)
JESUS	*Jesus is the better prophet because He is the very Word of God, and He always speaks the true words of His Father.* (John 1:1, 12:49)	*Jesus is a better priest because He offered up Himself as the perfect sacrifice and once-for-all atonement for our sins, and He is our High Priest forever.* (Hebrews 7:27–28)	*Jesus is a better king because He will reign on His throne in heaven forever, and there is nothing outside of His control.* (Revelation 19:13–16)

HE IS
EVER
FAITHFUL.

WHERE TO GO WITH EVERY WORRY

Read Lamentations 4:17–22

This segment of poem four is another corporate testimony that the poet gives on behalf of the people. In all the affliction that came upon Jerusalem, their first action was to look for help from the hands of other nations. This only confirmed their punishment because they should have called out to the Lord first. The Lord had pleaded with Jerusalem in Jeremiah 30:15 to return and rest in Him. If she had done so, she would have been saved. But the people chose to trust in other things like the nation of Egypt as their ally. But when Babylon invaded, Egypt was nowhere to be found. The original Hebrew repeats the word, watching, for emphasis in order to demonstrate the futility of Israel's efforts to save themselves. It only left their eyes weary from straining to see a help that would never come.

How often are we also tempted to turn to worldly allies before we ask the Lord for help? We call a friend to vent, read a book on the topic, spend our hours fretting, or turn on the television to turn off our brains before we even take a moment to bring the issue to the Lord in prayer. We make the same mistake as Jerusalem. Egypt could not save, and neither can any other worldly ally.

Because they would not rest in the Lord, Israel faced invasion instead of deliverance. They could not even walk in their own streets for fear of being beaten. This was the reality of siege warfare, and it appeared to be the end of the city. In verse 19, we hear that the people of Jerusalem tried to escape the city when the sieges began. They ran into the wilderness seeking protection for themselves, but their pursuers were too fast. Babylon hunted them down in the wilderness and took them as their captives.

In verse 20, the poet refers again to the king's death. The capture and killing of this leader was cause for no slight grief. The king of Israel is referred to as "the Lord's anointed" throughout Scripture because God appointed men to this position. The king's role was integral, and he himself was a sign of security for the people. But Israel had placed tremendous hope in the earthly king to save them instead of hoping in the one who appointed and preserved that king. But now that there was no ruler in Israel, there was virtually no hope for the continuation of that kingdom. The death of King Zedekiah was yet another sign of punishment and one which made it seem as though the Lord had utterly abandoned His people.

If Israel had looked to the Lord initially, they would have heard Him calling them to rest in Him, just like Jeremiah prophesied. They did not have to do anything but be still, and God would have fought for them. We tend to think that we have to do this or that to fix or change our situation, but often the Lord is just calling us to be still. There are certainly times when He calls us to action like He did with Esther or King David or many others. But so many other times, He just calls us to be still while He takes action on our behalf. Jerusalem did not have to go chasing other nations for allies; they did not even have to go into battle. The most primary calling they had, and one which we share, was to listen to and obey the Lord's voice.

If He calls us to action, then we go; if He calls us to stillness, then we rest. But either way, the constant calling we have is to seek the Lord and ask for His guidance. God can accomplish far more in our stillness than anything that we could ever do in all our efforts. But the point is not that we never take action. The point is that our first move should always be to approach God in prayer and seek Him in His Word. Our second action should be obedience to what He calls us to in those places.

The truth at the base of all our striving after worldly allies and aids is that we do not fully trust the Lord. Clearly, Jerusalem did not either. Our distrust of God in the day to day worries and struggles is surprising when we realize all that the Lord has already accomplished on our behalf. Think about what He did through Jesus: your sin is paid for, you have access to Father God, you will never face eternal death or punishment, you will reign with Christ for eternity in heaven, and nothing on earth below or above will change God's love for you. We have all this as believers, and yet sometimes we question whether the Lord will provide our basic, daily needs.

In Matthew 6:25–34, Jesus talks about anxiety and the human tendency to worry about things that the Lord has perfect control over. At the root of these things is a lack of trust in the Lord. Jesus's words bring the audience back to this truth: not only does our heavenly Father know our needs, but He cares for us more than He does for all the other creatures of the earth, whom He also provides for. If God is faithful to sustain birds that do not even plan for their next meal, how much more will He care for us, His own precious children, every moment?

These are the truths that Jerusalem did not believe, and they are the ones that Jesus came to proclaim in such a way that would enable us to receive them. He sent us His Holy Spirit so that when we struggle to believe God's words even today, He can guide us back into the truth. Your greatest need has been met in Christ Jesus. All you need now is to rest in His sufficient work. When the Lord does call you to action, it is not so that you can accomplish something in your own strength. The truth is that even when you have successful efforts in your action, it is God who gives the fruit. He is ever faithful like that, and we get to simply abide in Him.

WHAT DO YOU FIND YOURSELF PLACING HOPE OR TRUST IN APART FROM GOD?

READ PSALM 81. WHAT DID THE LORD OFFER TO ISRAEL IF THEY HAD LISTENED TO HIM AND OBEYED HIS VOICE?

READ JOHN 15:1–11. WHAT DOES IT LOOK LIKE TO ABIDE IN THE LORD? WHAT DOES THAT MEAN FOR YOUR DAY TODAY?

WE CAN
HOLD FAST
TO WHAT GOD
HAS DONE
THROUGH
JESUS.

THE DARKNESS IS NOT DARK WITH HIM

Read Lamentations 4:21–22 and Micah 7:8–10

As the chapter comes to a close, the introspective tone of first-person plural pronouns in verses 17–20 gives way to second person pronouns in the final stanzas of the poem. Verse 21 begins with the commands to rejoice and be glad. How can they rejoice? How can they be glad? Does the situation described in the previous verses call for celebration? As we read the rest of the line, we see that this command is given to Edom, not Jerusalem. While Babylon was the primary force in the massacre of God's people, Edom was a neighboring city that benefited from the attacks and may have assisted Babylon in some way. The tone of verse 21 is that Edom should rejoice while they still can. The metaphor of drinking from a cup is often used in Scripture to describe the Lord's wrath and judgment. Edom will one day have their fill of this drink (Ezekiel 36).

The Daughter of Zion has been drinking deeply from that cup for quite some time, but in verse 22 she reveals that the punishment is complete, and her people's exile will soon come to an end. The second line of verse 22 could read as if the punishment is over or as if it will end sometime soon. In a sense, it is both. As far as we know, Jerusalem was still in physical exile at the time that this poem was penned. Yet the poet has received some sign from the Lord indicating that Jerusalem's punishment is now complete. This is evidence that at least the spiritual exile has come to an end because clearly, God is communicating with His people again.

Just as Jerusalem has been uncovered and shamed, soon her enemies will feel the same reproach. In Micah 7:8–10, the prophet Micah speaks about this coming vindication of Israel. He is talking to his enemies now. The darkness that Micah sits in is likely a metaphor for a spiritual condition involving sin and the consequences that result from it like guilt, shame, and physical consequences. He says that when he is overwhelmed by those things, even then the Lord is a light to him. Even when his own sin has led him into the darkness and he has to bear the Lord's judgment, he is confident that the Lord Himself will come to plead his case against the enemy. He was right. In Ezekiel 36, the Lord speaks about His plan to champion Israel's cause. He says that He does not come for their sake though but rather, to fight for the glory of His name which Israel tarnished before the nations. We will hear more about what the Lord will do for Israel in the final poem.

In the meantime, Micah's prayer is a comfort during the wait for physical deliverance, even as Jerusalem begins to experience the blessings of spiritual restoration with the Lord. The dimness of dwelling among people who do not know the Lord in Babylon has caused a spiritual dryness that probably felt like a kind of depression. Micah acknowledges his guilt of sin in this passage and declares that it is right for him to endure punishment. But even as he suffers under the Lord's hand, the hope that gets him through the day is confidence that the Lord will also rescue and restore him. He cannot see it with his eyes yet because he is still in the darkness, so Micah says to himself about the Lord, "He will bring me into the light; I will see His salvation" (7:9). He reminded himself of the truth in the midst of spiritual discouragement. Guilt over our sin can leave a really heavy weight on our minds and hearts. The physical consequences that sometimes accompany it can make it challenging to believe in hope when circumstances seem hopeless. For Jerusalem, their ruined city and displaced family members were those physical realities.

Micah is really pointing forward to Christ without even knowing His name. The One who would come to be light and bring Micah and his people out of darkness was the One who called Himself the Light of the World (John 8:12). Jesus is referred to as light all throughout Scripture,

and the beautiful thing about this is that where He is, darkness cannot stay. This does not mean that as believers we will never experience shame over our sin or even seasons of depression where we face a strong feeling of darkness. But it does mean that if you are in Christ, the darkness can never define your identity. It means that even as you walk through dim valleys, His light is within you, and nothing can shake your salvation.

Before we knew Christ, we were filled with darkness because we were owned and defined by sin. Once we believed in Christ, He entered our hearts. Where He is, there cannot be any darkness at all (1 John 1:5). Maybe this seems confusing because as Christians, we still deal daily with indwelling sins. Are those not a kind of darkness? Yes, but if we belong to Christ, that sin does not have power over us because it does not own us anymore. This means that when we struggle with persistent sins or battle guilt over them, we can boldly say, "The Lord is a light to me; the Lord is my salvation." The prophet Micah had to cling to what God would do through the coming Savior, but we can hold fast to what God has done through Jesus already. We also have no need to feel ashamed; we are guilty of sin, but that sin has been covered by Jesus on the cross. Our sin does not define our identity anymore–Christ and His light do.

At the very end of this fourth poem in Lamentations, the poet proclaims victory in the midst of his suffering. As a kind Father, God disciplined Israel to train them, and soon He would scoop them up in His tender, fatherly arms to comfort them. Your enemy, the devil, still tries to shake you, but his weapons of sin and death have been disarmed by Jesus. One day in heaven there will be no darkness at all, even in our surroundings. But Jesus is light in us now, even while we wait and wrestle and look forward with the poet and the prophet to the complete redemption of all things.

READ THE FOLLOWING PASSAGES ABOUT JESUS. WHAT DOES IT MEAN THAT HE IS LIGHT?

JOHN 8:12

EPHESIANS 5:6–14

1 JOHN 1:5–2:2

READ 1 JOHN 1:5–2:2 AGAIN. HOW DOES THIS PASSAGE HELP US IF WE FEEL GUILT OVER SIN?

REMEMBER THAT GUILT AND SHAME ARE DIFFERENT. GUILT IS LIKE A THERMOMETER; IT REVEALS SIN SO THAT YOU CAN DEAL WITH IT. SHAME IS LIKE A THERMOSTAT; IT SAYS THAT YOU SHOULD FEEL LIKE SIN DEFINES AND CONDEMNS YOU. WHAT DOES THE PASSAGE YOU READ FROM 1 JOHN SAY ABOUT HOW TO DEAL WITH GUILT AND RESPOND TO SHAME?

LAMENTATIONS 3:24

I say, "The Lord is my portion, therefore I will put my hope in him."

Week Six Reflection

REVIEW LAMENTATIONS 3:59–4:22

Paraphrase the passage from this week.

_____

_____

_____

_____

_____

_____

_____

_____

_____

_____

_____

_____

_____

_____

What did you observe from this week's text about God and His character?

_____

_____

_____

_____

_____

_____

_____

What does this week's passage reveal about the condition of mankind and about yourself?

_____

_____

_____

How does this passage point to the gospel?

_____

_____

_____

_____

How should you respond to this passage? What is the personal application?

_____

_____

_____

_____

What specific action steps can you take this week to apply this passage?

_____

_____

_____

_____

THE BOOK OF
LAMENT IS
COMING TO
AN END, BUT
SALVATION IS
STILL ON THE
HORIZON.

GRACE AND DISGRACE

Read Lamentations 5:1–10

While there have been whispered prayers here and there and a few loud cries to the Lord throughout the book, this final poem is addressed entirely to God as a communal prayer. The first-person plural pronouns throughout identify that the poet is speaking on behalf of Jerusalem as a whole. The prayer will include a confession, a statement of need, an adoration of the Lord for His sovereignty, and a plea for Him to restore. This last poem mimics the 22-stanza pattern of the rest of the book, but it is not an acrostic. By breaking this literary pattern, there is a sense of closure. The book of lament is coming to an end, but salvation is still on the horizon. This prayer, which takes place on the boundary between grief and praise, begins with an introduction that guides us through the chapter: The poet calls the Lord once again to look and see His people's disgrace, but this time he asks God to specifically remember.

By asking Him to remember, the poet is not implying that God was experiencing amnesia. God has no memory limit, and He can hold every detail of the past, present, and future in His mind at once. But in Scripture, God remembering often signifies that He is going to act in redemptive ways. The poet is asking God to remember in accordance with the blessings of the covenant rather than what their sin deserves. He is requesting covenant redemption from God's hand, even though he and his people have grievously broken the covenant. And almost as though trying to help Him along in the remembering process, the prayer begins to confess Jerusalem's disgraceful condition again. The language of a broken covenant is used throughout these descriptions.

The first instance of covenant vocabulary is the word inheritance. As God's covenant people called out of slavery in Egypt, Israel was entitled to an inheritance of land, but now they were considered strangers to it, and instead, foreigners inhabited their homes. The Babylonians were strangers, not only geographically, but they were also outsiders to the covenant. Next, there is the covenant language of widow, orphan, and fatherless ones. God's law, which was given along with the land, had strong commands that Israel should care for these vulnerable people groups. It makes God angry when people are oppressed in a way that leaves them in such need. The irony is that part of Israel's punishment is that they themselves have become orphans, fatherless, and widowed, for treating these groups so harshly. In addition to this, there is also the loss of covenant provision. Now, each meal comes to them at the cost of their lives.

During the Exodus from Egypt many generations before, God led the people out into the wilderness. It had been a place of rest, provision, and nearness to the Lord through covenant bonds. In verse 9, the poet reveals that now the wilderness is a place of danger where the people meet the sword instead of manna from heaven. All of these subversions of the covenant must have left the people grief-stricken and nearly hopeless. This statement of their current condition is a kind of confession of their having broken the covenant bonds.

When the poet says that the people bear their parents' punishment, he is not trying to lay all the blame on previous generations as if he and his people are innocent. He has clearly testified throughout the book that he and the people have sinned greatly. God was patient and waited to bring judgment on Israel for many generations because of His merciful forbearance. Now, the people are indeed bearing the weight of the judgment for several generations. But they are not the victims of other people's sin; they are the rightful bearers of just, covenantal punishment.

The Lord is so faithful to this covenant that even when the people break it and He has every right to completely abandon them, He again and again shows mercy. In fact, the Lord's compassion is so great that not only would He rescue disgraced Israel through Christ's work, but by sending Jesus He would also invite people from every nation to receive salvation through Him. Paul says in Ephesians 3:6 that this gift of salvation to the Gentiles who are those outside of ethnic Israel is a mystery that was hidden during the Old Testament. The promise of the Messiah was made to ethnic Israel through covenant bonds thousands of years ago, but because of God's great love for the world, all have been invited to inherit this promise too. Because Jesus fulfilled the covenant law perfectly and received the inheritance, those who have faith in Him receive the blessings too.

As Jerusalem enjoyed renewed communication with God while remaining in physical exile, they would learn that the covenant had always been about a relationship with God. It was never meant to be about the temporal benefits. Today we live on a similar boundary between spiritual deliverance and physical rescue. This world is a kind of exile for those who know Jesus. We are strangers here because heaven is our home. But God has sent the Holy Spirit into our hearts now so that we can have a restored relationship with God and become more and more like Christ while we wait for the fullness of our inheritance in heaven.

This is a challenging tension to endure, especially as we face the brokenness of this world. But our joy was never supposed to be found in this world alone. So even though things are broken and that rightly grieves us, we can still have joy because we will never lose the only thing with eternal significance. A relationship with the God of the universe is the sole source of lasting joy because in it, you will find your identity and purpose. It is what Israel temporarily lost but desperately needed. It was what God was seeking to restore in them. And it is what Christ has secured for you by His work.

You can deepen your relationship with the Lord daily by reading His Word and spending time in prayer, talking to Him. We will spend eternity dwelling with the Lord physically, and we get to prepare for that endless glory now through daily habits of partaking in His grace.

READ PSALM 74 ABOUT THE DESTRUCTION OF JERUSALEM. HOW IS THE PSALMIST WRITING FROM THE SAME BOUNDARY BETWEEN GRIEF AND PRAISE?

IS YOUR OWN LIFE TOUCHED BY PHYSICAL OR TEMPORAL SUFFERING? HOW DOES CHRIST'S WORK GIVE YOU HOPE AND CALL YOU TO WORSHIP IN THE MIDST OF IT?

READ EPHESIANS 4:17–32. HOW ARE YOU CALLED TO LIVE IN LIGHT OF YOUR NEW LIFE IN CHRIST?

IS HIS JUSTICE LATE?
Read Lamentations 5:11–15 and Jeremiah 31:1–20

Reading the two passages for today may have felt jolting because of their contrasting tones. Lamentations continues the prayer poem with horrific descriptions of the suffering that each social class of Jerusalem has experienced. Jeremiah 31 records God's words to these oppressed people and the complete restoration that will come for them. It is not easy to read Lamentations 5, but it may have felt even more challenging to see it beside the sweet promises of Jeremiah 31. They are good and life-giving and so abundantly merciful beyond anything Israel could have ever hoped to receive after their wretched sin. But none of that changes the present reality of what Jerusalem has endured and what they are still experiencing as the poet writes his prayer.

Women are defenseless and vulnerable to sexual violation and humiliation against their will. This not only disgraces them, but it also shames the men who should have been there to protect them. But those men could not help because they were being tortured and killed, hung up by their hands. The people are slaves, and the Babylonians have put even their little ones to forced labor. Children literally crumble under the weight of work that they are too small to bear. The elders' absence in the gate is a sign of economic deconstruction and the breakdown of civilization. The people's hearts are filled with despair and pain. Not only are their lungs too weak, but their souls are so discouraged that they likely would not know what words to sing even if they could.

These descriptions should sound familiar to us. Sexual violence, modern slavery, human trafficking, child-labor, fragmented social orders, broken families, and economic disparity haunt virtually every corner of the globe today. The reality of these things is appalling, and it should break our hearts even if none of these horrors reflect our own personal experience. We can and should speak the truth that God will redeem all things one day — every sorted sin and treacherous action. Justice will come in the form of vengeance on the wicked that only God can bring in a truly just way. But we cannot say only that. We are called to live justly now and to fight on behalf of our fellow image-bearers when they suffer injustice in the meantime (Micah 6:8).

It is tempting to question God at this point in our prayers. And it is okay to do so. The Psalms are filled with these kinds of prayers. The psalmists brought their questions to God, talked through them with Him, and they clung to God's character as they did so. They did not accuse Him, but they were honest about how life felt from their perspective. Sometimes God's justice may seem delayed from our viewpoint, but He is never late. He cares for our earthly sufferings, but His greatest concern is for our eternal condition.

The same tension that we feel as we read today's passages is present throughout Jesus's life and ministry. There is an example in John 11 when Jesus raises a man named Lazerus from the dead. Lazarus had two sisters named Mary and Martha who called for Jesus when Lazerus was ill, asking Him to come and heal their brother. Jesus was a few day's journey away, but rather than leaving immediately, he waited several days. When He arrived, Lazarus had already been dead for four days, and Jesus knew this before He even came to visit.

When they speak with Jesus, Mary and Martha seem to be wrestling with the same kinds of questions that we have asked while reading Lamentations. They both tell Him, "Lord, if you had been here, my brother would not have died!" The women knew that Jesus's power was great, and they did not understand why He had not used it to prevent this grievous thing from taking place. Even the crowds who came to comfort the family questioned Jesus's timing. We know that Jesus soon raised Lazarus from the dead in spite of all their doubting. But possibly the most surprising thing about this passage is what Jesus does after he is told that Lazerus is dead and before He does His miraculous work. Jesus begins to weep (John 11:35). He was about to fix everything by raising Lazarus from the dead, but still He weeps in the in between.

Jesus wept because death is a result of sin and was not part of God's original design for creation. It is a product of the curse that began when sin entered the world, and every result of the fall grieves the Lord. While God has always planned to redeem and restore all elements that our sin has touched, that does not change the fact that the damage has occurred. If God Himself wept over those things, then there is a place for us to do so as well. But just as God's grief over sin is never separated from His power and plan to restore, then neither should be our sorrow. So how do we respond to realities in our world today like those described in Lamentations 5? We weep, just like Jesus. We ask Him questions, and like Mary and Martha did, we ask Him to heal. And when His answer does not come in the timing we expected, we trust that His ways are higher and that His glory will shine.

God sees the pain that sin has personally caused you as well. He sent His own Son to be mocked, reviled, and crucified in order to heal you from it. Though we may never fully grasp this reality until heaven, the joy and peace that are coming cannot even compare with the present suffering (Romans 8:18). This does not minimize the very real brokenness present in the world. Murder, rape, slavery, abuse, neglect, hunger, sadness, and death are real and present and worthy of godly sorrow. But you can cling to the truth that not even a shadow of this sorrow will exist when we are raised up in heaven with new bodies, sitting right beside Jesus, and praising His name forever and ever. You will be perfectly sinless and completely satisfied, as will everyone around you. So as you wait, a practical practice is to immerse yourself in God's Word by reading through the book of Psalms filled with the prayers and songs of those who have walked in this shattered world and which testify to God's faithful, redeeming work through the ages.

READ LUKE 11. WHAT DOES THIS PASSAGE REVEAL ABOUT GOD'S CHARACTER?

READ ROMANS 8:18–30. WHAT HELP AND HOPE DO YOU HAVE AS YOU WAIT EAGERLY WITH PATIENCE IN A WORLD THAT IS GROANING UNDER THE WEIGHT OF SIN?

HOW HAVE YOU WITNESSED SIN BRING PAIN INTO YOUR OWN LIFE AND INTO THE WORLD? SPEND SOME TIME TALKING TO THE LORD IN PRAYER ABOUT THESE THINGS, ASKING HIM TO HELP YOU SEE HIS COMPASSION AND JUSTICE IN THESE SITUATIONS.

GOD CONTINUALLY CALLS HIS PEOPLE TO FAITH AND REPENTANCE THROUGHOUT SCRIPTURE.

FAITH AND REPENTANCE

Read Lamentations 5:16–18

God continually calls His people to faith and repentance throughout Scripture. But both of these things are somewhat foreign concepts in modern culture. Maybe it is because they have one, central thing in common—both require humility. It takes humility to repent because it means confessing that you are not perfect. And it takes humility to have faith because it means that you have to rely on something or someone other than yourself. Humans have instead sought autonomy ever since the garden of Eden when Adam and Eve did not want to trust God's word by faith. The downward spiral into prideful, pseudo-independence has continued throughout history.

Just as Adam and Eve thought they knew better than God, so Jerusalem pridefully pursued independence from Him. But they did not realize that everything that made them feel powerful had come from God's hand. The dignity, honor, and respect that they had before other nations were due to God's provision, protection, and the presence of His name in their midst. Now, the crown of that honor has fallen from their heads. The second line in verse 16 is one of the strongest signs of repentance we hear in the book: "Woe to us, for we have sinned." The people finally seem to understand that the connection between their trials and their transgressions is that sin leads to death and destruction every time (Romans 6:23).

Maybe that is a sign of repentance, but is there faith present here? Verses 17 and 18 seem hopeless. The people are weary from crying, and their hearts are sick, probably from being disappointed over and over again. The physical land of Jerusalem is a constant, visual reminder and representation of their spiritual condition. Mount Zion, the place where God's own glory was supposed to dwell, is in ruins. Every crevice of the city is leveled to the ground. From all external appearances, Jerusalem and its people are shattered beyond repair. But this was God. The nation of Israel was called an unshakable city (Psalm 125:1). Clearly it has been shaken, so were all of those promises false? How do we know that the people still have faith in them?

Prayer. Chapter 5 is a prayer. Not only this, but it is a prayer addressed to God. In spite of what their eyes see in the city and in exile, the people of Jerusalem still have faith in God. See, the beauty of faith is that it is not based on what is physically visible. The Bible says in the book of Hebrews that "faith is the reality of what is hoped for, the proof of what is not seen" (Hebrews 11:1). Even though the present does not look like the past, the people have faith based on who God has previously proven Himself to be. So though it is terrible to behold, the dim vision of the city does not sway their ultimate confidence because their faith is no longer based on the temporal but on the eternal One.

Faith is evidenced by their prayer but also by their repentance. When we repent of our sin, it means that we are not only admitting our failure, but we are also asking God for the strength to change so that we do not continue to sin in that particular way. Thus, this glimmer of repentance in the poet's prayer is a sign that the people of Jerusalem are not only acknowledging their sin against the Lord, but they also have faith to ask Him for change.

Repentance is a sign that the people of Israel finally have faith in the right thing. Before their punishment, they had faith in idols made by their hands and in other nations. They likely put their faith in those things because it was easier to cling to what they could see. Now that their faith is in God, they recognize that their sins were against Him and require repentance. We too are often tempted to put our trust in earthly things or people instead of in God. But truly, that is not faith because those things are visible. True faith is challenging to hold onto because we cannot see the thing that we cling to. This is why God sent Jesus.

Because of Christ, the size of our faith does not matter because it is placed in our strong Savior.

Both repentance and faith are gifts from God that we receive through Christ. Our faith looks differently than that of God's people in Jerusalem during the exile. They looked forward to the Messiah who would come to save them, even if they were not alive when He arrived. God's word had to be enough for them, and their faith in Jesus's future work made them righteous before God. We have Jesus's finished work as the fodder for our faith today. As Hebrews 11:1 says, our faith is the evidence that Jesus will come again one day to fulfill our hope for eternal restoration. Israel's sins were awful, and their outlook on the future was dim, but the truth is that the same kind of evil can be found everywhere in the world today. When sin entered the garden of Eden, it permeated all of creation. Jesus died once for all to deal with this sin and give the free gifts of faith and repentance to all who believe in Him.

Until He returns to end sin forever, we still need the faith and repentance that He gives because it is not easy to live in this world and hold on to hope sometimes. Faith is necessary because you are counted righteous before God on the basis of your faith in Him, not in your works. And repentance is needed because your sin continues. We need to daily confess our sin and ask the Lord for forgiveness and the power to help us turn away from it. As we are sanctified in this way, the Lord is preparing our hearts for heaven where faith and repentance will give way to sight and perfect praise. In the meantime, even if your own sight feels dim, remember that what Jesus has won, He cannot lose. Your salvation is secure even if your faith feels weak.

READ ROMANS 4. WHY IS FAITH
NECESSARY?

READ ROMANS 5:1–5. HOW IS FAITH AN
ANCHOR IN YOUR AFFLICTIONS?

ARE THEIR SINS THAT YOU HAVE BEEN STRUGGLING WITH LATELY?
SPEND SOME TIME IN PRAYER, CONFESSING THESE TO THE LORD AND
ASKING HIM TO TURN YOUR AFFECTIONS AWAY FROM THOSE SINS
AND MORE TOWARD HIM.

THAT IS
THE POINT OF
GRACE — WE
DO NOT
DESERVE IT.

A HEART THAT ONLY GOD CAN CHANGE

Read Lamentations 5:19–22 and Ezekiel 36

The poet moved from the lowly, desolate situation in Jerusalem in verse 18 where there was a dim view of the future, to the intensely high and hopeful stance of verse 19. From the people's own mouths there is a confirmation that they have faith in God who is on His throne. Even though Jerusalem is in ruins and the earthly temple has been destroyed, God's throne cannot be shaken. He will reign forever, and no amount of earthly turmoil can remove Him from that rule. For a while, the people likely felt as though Babylon was the ultimate power over them, but now they recognize that not even their captors could control their future, only the Lord has that power.

Verse 20 returns to the reality of Jerusalem's present experience. God is on the throne, but they are still suffering. The people wonder and question whether the Lord will leave them as they are for all time, because they know that He is the one in control of their lives. Their rhetorical questions, asking if the Lord had forgotten them, can be answered by Isaiah 49:15 when the Lord says to His people, "Can a woman forget her nursing child, or lack compassion for the child of her womb? Even if these forget, yet I will not forget you." Israel is still God's child. They may be wayward, but He parents them nonetheless, and He will never forget them. If we are in Christ, we are God's children too, which means the same promise applies to us (Hebrews 13:5).

In verse 21, the poet reveals the people's greatest need. Clearly, they require restoration, but something needs to be done in order for that restoration to take place. Israel needs to be restored. It is not as simple as the people deciding to turn back to the Lord; they need to be brought back. Their role is passive, not active. If they pursue restoration on their own, it may last for a season, but they can never purify themselves from sin, so they would certainly fail and fall again into a damaged relationship with

God. This is why the poet says that Jerusalem and her people need to be brought back by God in order to be able to return. God must initiate the restoration. God promises to restore them to a right covenant relationship, for the glory of His name throughout the earth, by giving them new hearts and His very own Spirit (Ezekiel 36).

Israel has proven incapable of following God because of their sinful condition, which is the same struggle that we faced before knowing Christ. This is why God promises to give them hearts that are capable of faith and obedience (Ezekiel 36:26). He would carry this out through Jesus who fulfilled God's covenant perfectly as we could not. When we trusted in Jesus for salvation, God gave us a new heart and His Spirit to dwell within us. Our faith is part of the fulfillment of God's promises in Ezekiel 36. The people of Jerusalem needed forgiveness which can only come through the shedding of blood for sacrifice (Hebrews 9:22). Just like Israel, we could not cleanse ourselves from sin, so Christ came and made us and the people of Jerusalem clean by His own perfect, sacrificial blood.

In Joel 2:13, the prophet addresses this heart-renewal. He tells the people that they do not need only to mourn outwardly by tearing their garments and acting sorry for their actions. They also need to demonstrate actual, inward change in their hearts. This is something that only God could bring about in them and in us. In Jeremiah 31:31–34, the Lord says that He would do this by writing His law on the hearts of the people. He would change them in ways that they could never change themselves, just as He has done for us, through Jesus.

The evidence that the Lord has begun this work is clear in verse 22. In its somber tone, Israel acknowledges that the Lord has cause to totally destroy them and to refuse to give the restoration they requested. Their hope and prayer is that He would remember them and show mercy through salvation, but they recognize the real penalty that their sin deserves. The Lord had declared this disaster long before through the prophets, but they had stopped their ears. Now they remember His words and see the righteousness of His judgments. They do not yet realize the tangible signs of a restored, covenantal relationship. They can only plead that God would bring it about and resign themselves to the fact that if He does not, He is still just.

As we read their words, our minds might think of Christ and how He fulfilled all their pleas through His life, death, and resurrection. But from Israel's perspective, that work was still to come. Yet, they waited in hope that God would be merciful. They were painfully aware that they did not deserve any of it and were fearful that the Lord would refuse to give it because of how far they had fallen.

We may feel tempted at times to look at our past and the weight of our sins and think that God cannot or will not accept us because of that baggage. Perhaps He would think it was too much or that we had fallen too far from His grace to deserve restoration. The truth is that whether we are the lowest criminal or the most pious church member, our sin is so wretched that there is nothing we could ever do to merit redemption. God did not come to rescue only those whose sin was not that bad. He came to die for sinners because their sin was that bad. That is the point of grace — we do not deserve it. His sacrifice is the only thing that could ever save both the criminals and the pious people, and He knew it. We are not too far from His grace, no matter how undeserving we may feel. That is just mercy.

READ HEBREWS 9. HOW IS THE NEW COVENANT BETTER THAN THE OLD?

WHAT IS THE DIFFERENCE BETWEEN OUTWARD SYMBOLS OF CHANGE AND GENUINE REPENTANCE? WHY DO WE NEED BOTH?

THE DEPTH OF OUR SIN DOES NOT MATTER WHEN IT COMES TO WHO GOD CAN REDEEM. WHAT DOES THIS TELL YOU ABOUT THE NATURE OF YOUR SALVATION?

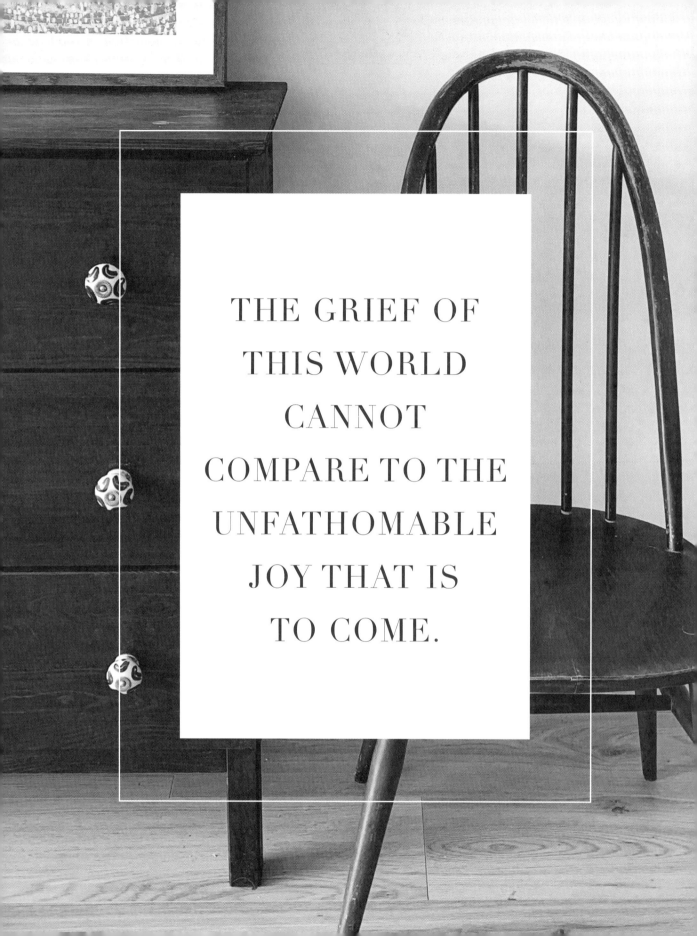

THE GRIEF OF
THIS WORLD
CANNOT
COMPARE TO THE
UNFATHOMABLE
JOY THAT IS
TO COME.

THE WAIT IN-BETWEEN
Read Isaiah 40 and Revelation 21

Lamentations is a book written in the middle of suffering and strife, but it is also a book that looks forward to the future on every page. It was written after the tragedy of Jerusalem but before the deliverance that would come. Along with every hopeful word, there is a call to wait. The book of Isaiah was written many years before the siege and exile of Jerusalem, and as we have seen, the prophet Isaiah revealed a great deal of information to Jerusalem about their punishment. But he also spoke about the future salvation, prophesying beyond their present pain.

In Isaiah 40, we hear the Lord's own words speaking peace to His people once again. We know now that the voice mentioned in verse 3 is John the Baptist who would come to prepare the way for Jesus's arrival and earthly ministry. And the glory that would be revealed is the coming of God's own Son into the world. When God the Son came, the rest of the chapter tells us that He would be revealed as a Good Shepherd, sovereign ruler, bearer of justice, infinite deity, a God far beyond comparison with any false idol made by human hands, and the Creator of the ends of the earth. But again, the chapter ends with a call again to wait for this One.

Though the wait would be long for Jerusalem, He promises that those who waited patiently for Christ would not grow weary or lose their faith (Isaiah 40:31). We have never had to wait for our salvation in the same way because we live on the other side of their wait. Jesus has come, and we have His revelation in Scripture and His Spirit to remind us of His words. Many of Isaiah's prophecies have been fulfilled long before our lifetime, but not all of them. We still wait for Jesus, not for His first coming but for His return. We have heard a great deal about this wait throughout our study.

All of the grand promises for complete restoration that we see throughout Scripture have only partially begun in our lifetime. They have been inaugurated in Christ, which means that He began them, but they have not yet been completely fulfilled. Even though thousands of years would pass in which His promises would come to fulfillment, He said on the cross, "It is finished" (John 19:30). He was referring to the work of our salvation that He came to earth to accomplish. In that moment, it was complete, and someday we will experience that completeness.

After He said these words, Jesus died and was buried in a tomb. From all earthly appearances, the only thing finished was Jesus's life. Jesus died and was raised. He could have hopped down from the cross or raised Himself right after being buried. But He did neither of those things, and His people had to live through the period from the time He died to His resurrection. It is so common in our lives to look at waiting as the purposeless obstacle between us and our goals or hopes. But God never wastes anything. He was doing work even in the in-between.

When the waiting was over, the morning revealed an empty tomb and the risen Savior. Thousands of years would follow in which people would come to a saving knowledge of Jesus. But in many ways the wait has still not ended, neither for Jerusalem nor for us. From God's perspective, all the work was fully accomplished when Jesus breathed His last on the cross because God is outside of time. Now, like a bride eagerly waiting for her groom, we, as the church, are being made ready for a marriage ceremony with Christ (Ephesians 5:27). In this sense, periods when we are waiting are not so that God has time to accomplish His purposes. When God creates waiting, it is always for our sake, to complete the work He wants to do in our lives that is often best accomplished in the in-between.

While it is full of hope for the Savior, it is also tinged by the grief that judgment brought. Lamentations was written in a period of waiting between distress and praise. Now, we face a similar paradox. Jesus has come, and our confidence in His return is certain, but this world is full of pain and sorrow. We know that each heartache will not only be soothed someday but will be undone. Revelation 21 speaks again of a restoration like the one in Isaiah 40. Truly, both of these chapters point to the same Savior and the same glorious, heavenly kingdom, even though they were written hundreds of years apart by two different men.

It can be challenging to live our lives in this long period of waiting that holds pain and troubles. The disciples experienced that reality in the strongest sense when Jesus died. They had the promise from Jesus's own lips that He would rise again, but they struggled to believe it during the period of waiting. Jerusalem had promises from God's mouth as well, and they wrestled to cling to them in the wait. We have the certain hope of Christ's return and the promise of an end to all sadness, sickness, and sin in heaven, and yet it can be challenging to trust the Lord in the midst of present sorrow and pain that seems unceasing. We fight darkness, doubt, and discouragement, and we pray with the author of Revelation that Jesus would return soon to fully restore His bride (Revelation 22:17). This pattern that we see all throughout history is the experience of the things that are already accomplished by God but that are not yet visible to our eyes.

So as you wait, cling to what you already have — Christ. Jesus is called the Word in Scripture for a reason. His words and His life fill the pages of your Bible, and He is speaking directly to you in them. As you read in Isaiah 40:8, "The Word of our God remains forever." God gave you His enduring word in a book so that you would have the testimonies of His faithfulness for an anchor. He also provided the community of the church, where believers can strive and grow together toward more fully reflecting Jesus in the interim period. The church as a whole, Christ's bride, partakes in the promise of being made perfect. The grief of this world cannot compare to the unfathomable joy that is to come.

READ EPHESIANS 5:22–33. HOW DOES CHRIST CLEANSE HIS BRIDE?

ARE THERE THINGS IN YOUR LIFE THAT PARTICULARLY REMIND YOU THAT WE ARE LIVING IN A SEASON OF WAITING? HOW MIGHT THE LORD BE USING THESE THINGS TO PREPARE YOU FOR THE DAY WHEN CHRIST RETURNS?

WHAT DO THESE PASSAGES REVEAL ABOUT GOD'S CHARACTER?

LAMENTATIONS 3:19–24

*Remember my affliction
and my homelessness, the
wormwood and the poison.
I continually remember them
and have become depressed.
Yet I call this to mind, and
therefore I have hope:
Because of the Lord's faithful
love we do not perish, for his
mercies never end. They are
new every morning; great is
your faithfulness! I say, "The
Lord is my portion, therefore
I will put my hope in him."*

Week Seven Reflection

REVIEW LAMENTATIONS 5:1–22

Paraphrase the passage from this week.

_____
_____
_____
_____
_____
_____
_____
_____
_____
_____
_____
_____
_____
_____
_____

What did you observe from this week's text about God and His character?

_____
_____
_____
_____
_____
_____

What does this week's passage reveal about the condition of mankind and about yourself?

_____

_____

_____

_____

How does this passage point to the gospel?

_____

_____

_____

_____

How should you respond to this passage? What is the personal application?

_____

_____

_____

_____

What specific action steps can you take this week to apply this passage?

_____

_____

_____

_____

EXTRA
RESOURCES

THE SUFFERING THAT BRINGS PEACE

— Reference Week 1, Day 5 —

There are many parallels in Lamentations and Isaiah 53 between the suffering that the people of Jerusalem experience and that of Christ, the suffering servant in Isaiah. Jesus was truly a man acquainted with sorrow and no stranger to our temporal pain. We can see both in the prophecy of Isaiah as well as in the rest of Scripture's record, that Jesus's suffering accomplished tremendous blessings such as salvation from sin and eternal life. Jerusalem's suffering, on the other hand, earned them nothing but shame. Just as He is the better servant of the Lord, Jesus is also the better sufferer on our behalf

	JERUSALEM	THE SUFFERING SERVANT
DESPISED BY MEN	*Lamentations 2:15*	*Isaiah 53:3*
MARRED IN APPEARANCE	*Lamentations 4:8*	*Isaiah 53:2*
BEARING PUNISHMENT	*Lamentations 1:8*	*Isaiah 53:5*
SUFFERING OPPRESSION	*Lamentations 1:10*	*Isaiah 53:7*
CAST OUT OF THE CAMP	*Lamentations 1:3*	*Isaiah 53:8*

PROPHECIES
CONFIRMED / FULFILLED

A CITY IS DESTROYED

Jeremiah 52 $\rightarrow$ Lamentations 1

JUDAH IS TAKEN INTO EXILE

Jeremiah 52:27 $\rightarrow$ Lamentations 1:3

GATES OF JERUSALEM
ARE DESTROYED

Jeremiah 14:2 $\rightarrow$ Lamentations 1:4

JERUSALEM WILL SUFFER
BECAUSE OF HER GREAT SIN

Jeremiah 13:22 $\rightarrow$ Lamentations 1:9

ISRAEL SHALL BECOME SLAVES
OF THEIR ENEMIES

Deuteronomy 28:48 $\rightarrow$ Lamentations 1:14

JERUSALEM WILL BE FILLED
WITH MOURNING AND LAMENT

Isaiah 29:2 $\rightarrow$ Lamentations 2:5

LEADERS REMOVED
FROM JERUSALEM

Hosea 3:4 $\rightarrow$ Lamentations 4:7–9, 20

FALSE PROPHETS WILL GIVE
FALSE PROPHECIES

Jeremiah 5:31 $\rightarrow$ Lamentations 2:14

JERUSALEM WILL EXPERIENCE
THE CURSES FOR DISOBEDIENCE
OF THE COVENANT

Deuteronomy 28:15–68 $\rightarrow$ Lamentations 2:17

ISRAEL WILL LEARN TO
WAIT ON THE LORD

Micah 7:7, Isaiah 30:18 $\rightarrow$ Lamentations 3:25–27

JERUSALEM'S ENEMIES
WILL BE PUNISHED

Jeremiah 49:15–16 $\rightarrow$ Lamentations 4:21–22

THE PATH OF EXILE

The route from Jerusalem to Babylon

. . . .

DISTANCE: 1678.2 MILES

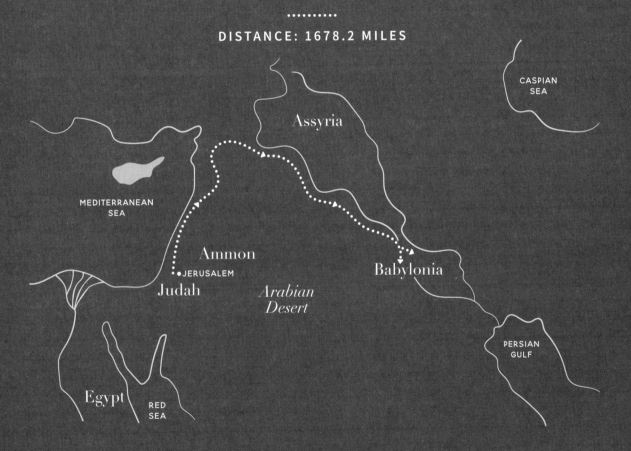

What is *the Gospel*?

Thank you for reading and enjoying this study with us! We are abundantly grateful for the Word of God, the instruction we glean from it, and the ever-growing understanding it provides for us of God's character. We are also thankful that Scripture continually points to one thing in innumerable ways: the gospel.

We remember our brokenness when we read about the fall of Adam and Eve in the garden of Eden (Genesis 3), where sin entered into a perfect world and maimed it. We remember the necessity that something innocent must die to pay for our sin when we read about the atoning sacrifices in the Old Testament. We read that we have all sinned and fallen short of the glory of God (Romans 3:23) and that the penalty for our brokenness, the wages of our sin, is death (Romans 6:23). We all need grace and mercy, but most importantly, we all need a Savior.

We consider the goodness of God when we realize that He did not plan to leave us in this dire state. We see His promise to buy us back from the clutches of sin and death in Genesis 3:15. And we see that promise accomplished with Jesus Christ on the cross. Jesus Christ knew no sin yet became sin so that we might become righteous through His sacrifice (2 Corinthians 5:21). Jesus was tempted in every way that we are and lived sinlessly. He was reviled yet still yielded Himself for our sake, that we may have life abundant in Him. Jesus lived the perfect life that we could not live and died the death that we deserved.

The gospel is profound yet simple. There are many mysteries in it that we will never understand this side of heaven, but there is still overwhelming weight to its implications in this life. The gospel tells of our sinfulness and God's goodness and a gracious gift that compels a response. We are saved by grace through faith, which means that we rest with faith in the grace that Jesus Christ displayed on the cross (Ephesians 2:8–9). We cannot save ourselves from our brokenness or do any amount of good works to merit God's favor. Still, we can have faith that what Jesus accomplished in His death, burial, and resurrection was more than enough for our salvation and our eternal delight. When we accept God, we are commanded to die to ourselves and our sinful desires and live a life worthy of the calling we have received (Ephesians 4:1). The gospel compels us to be sanctified, and in so doing, we are conformed to the likeness of Christ Himself. This is hope. This is redemption. This is the gospel.

GENESIS 3:15

I will put hostility between you and the woman, and between your offspring and her offspring. He will strike your head, and you will strike his heel.

ROMANS 3:23

For all have sinned and fall short of the glory of God.

ROMANS 6:23

For the wages of sin is death, but the gift of God is eternal life in Christ Jesus our Lord.

2 CORINTHIANS 5:21

He made the one who did not know sin to be sin for us, so that in him we might become the righteousness of God.

EPHESIANS 2:8–9

For you are saved by grace through faith, and this is not from yourselves; it is God's gift—not from works, so that no one can boast.

EPHESIANS 4:1–3

Therefore I, the prisoner in the Lord, urge you to walk worthy of the calling you have received, with all humility and gentleness, with patience, bearing with one another in love, making every effort to keep the unity of the Spirit through the bond of peace.

Thank you for studying
God's Word with us!

CONNECT WITH US
@thedailygraceco
@dailygracepodcast

CONTACT US
info@thedailygraceco.com

SHARE
#thedailygraceco

VISIT US ONLINE
www.thedailygraceco.com

MORE DAILY GRACE
Daily Grace® Podcast